Beyond Imagination

A New Reality Awaits

~∽⧼∾~

Elsie Spittle

Also written by Elsie Spittle
Wisdom for Life
Our True Identity. . . Three Principles

Beyond Imagination

A New Reality Awaits

⁓⁕⁓

Elsie Spittle

3 Principles for Human Development
www.3phd.net

About the Author

Elsie Spittle has been an internationally recognized trainer and consultant for almost four decades. She is one of the few people who knew Sydney Banks, originator of the Three Principles, before he had his profound insight, and who steadfastly supported him, despite her early strong resistance to his message. Elsie had the privilege of receiving "on the job" training directly from Mr. Banks, and was the first teacher, other than Syd, to share the Principles with mental health practitioners, educators, and others seeking a deeper understanding of life.

Over the years, Elsie has worked with all levels of executives and employees in the corporate world, and has helped transform disadvantaged communities. She considered it a privilege to work with staff and youth in juvenile justice settings. She is in demand as a public speaker, at conferences as well as on webinars, and continues to work with individuals via coaching and private mentoring programs. Elsie is co-founder of the Three Principles School, dedicated to sharing the integrity and purity of the Principles for the benefit of future generations.

In this book, Elsie Spittle shares stories of the early evolution of the Three Principles. She describes their emergence into many fields of human endeavor, particularly the mental health field. She tells of her own on-going learning as she points people, from all walks of life, to the natural, innate wisdom within.

This collection of heartfelt, true stories draws the reader into a world of hope and inspiration. Elsie tells of executives and employees learning to bring out the best in each other, where they thrive rather than survive. She tells of families facing heart wrenching challenges and coming through with grace and dignity. She also shares her own journey of discovering a reality beyond her imagination. Syd told her she would travel the world sharing the message of hope and transformation, if she *heard* him. Elsie listened to these words with disbelief—but the unbelievable happened.

Ms. Spittle has also written *Wisdom for Life,* and *Our True Identity.*

She can be reached via her website: www.3phd.net (3 Principles for Human Development).

What People Are Saying About
Beyond Imagination

In *Beyond Imagination* Elsie Spittle shares her improbable journey from housewife to international consultant. Elsie's sharing of the Three Universal Principles, as revealed to her friend Sydney Banks, is done with clarity, warmth, elegance and ease.

Reading this book will awaken many souls to their "true identity" and an experience of peace. From that perspective, Elsie's vision of world peace looks not only possible, but likely.

William F. Pettit Jr. MD,
Co-owner Three Principles Intervention LLC,
Former Associate Professor of Psychiatry,
West Virginia University School of Medicine

⁓ꝗꝗ⁓

Elsie's book tells of her ongoing journey of learning about the Three Principles, as Sydney Banks taught her through his words and actions. She shares how this journey has provided an ever-deepening awareness of her own inner health and wisdom, and gently guides readers to discover insights, from within themselves. I have been fortunate to attend talks given by Elsie, and can truly say that *reading the words in this book are as powerful as hearing her speak.*

Lynanne Lawhead, Executive Director,
Cypress Center for Well-Being

⁓ꝗꝗ⁓

Beyond Imagination offers readers a unique glimpse into the earliest history of The Three Principles, as awareness of their profound impact grew and began to spread throughout the world.

Elsie Spittle has been a pioneering practitioner in a wide range of areas. This book offers the reader the best of Elsie. You get a sense of her sweetness and caring and her outlook on life.

You can see and feel the influence of Sydney Banks in the flow, feel and focus of the book and it is lovely to see that live on with us through Elsie's work. This book has a lot to offer people new to the Principles understanding, as well as those who want to keep learning more. Thank you, Elsie, for taking the time to share all of this with us.

**Aaron Turner Ph.D., Co-founder and senior partner,
One Thought Ltd.**

❧

As I read this book, I felt myself calming inside, becoming quieter, relaxed and deeply peaceful—aware of how much I love ALL of life. I know these beautiful feelings are the core of who I am, who we all are. With humility, clarity and amazing grace, Elsie reminds us that the antidote to personal and professional overwhelm is within reach—it is inside, at the core of our being. Every organization I have ever worked for or with, every student I have ever had the privilege to teach and every person I have ever counseled, coached, befriended or loved has been searching for the TRUTH expressed in "Beyond Imagination".

**Linda Sandel Pettit, Ed.D., Dean of Graduate College,
Assistant Professor, Counselor Education,
Siena Heights University, Adrian, MI**

❧

Those of us who have grown to appreciate Elsie Spittle's wisdom and common sense will be excited about her latest book, *Beyond Imagination*. Once again she relates lessons from her personal journey and discoveries, helping us access our own compassion, confidence and understanding of happiness. The realization that we all have the ability to create our experience and tap into an inner wisdom that can guide our thoughts, feelings and actions is a valuable gift. This book is a "must read" for anybody interested in developing new insights about their personal and professional relationships.

Peter Debreceny, Strategy Execution Consultant, Chicago

I have been a student and teacher of the Three Principles understanding for over 20 years and was surprised at how much I learned from reading this book. I was deeply touched by the simplicity, openness and depth of feeling conveyed. I have had wonderful insights reading these chapters and find myself experiencing more calm and peace of mind, as well as a simpler perspective on my mind, than before.

Ken Manning, Ph.D., President of Insight Principles and licensed psychologist

Beyond Imagination is a magical story of the power of love and well-being to transform anyone. I found myself tearing up as I read Elsie's description of Syd and how she changed just being in the presence of such a deep level of consciousness. The feeling coming through her words is very sweet and yet powerful; it has the potential to touch the reader in the same way she was touched by the feeling Syd shared.

The insight that prompted Elsie's change was striking in its simplicity, and her stories show that we can all achieve this kind of transformation. *Beyond Imagination* is truly inspirational, bringing hope in the message that each of us has an unlimited potential for wisdom and happiness, within.

Christine J. Heath, LMFT Hawaii/Minnesota Counseling and Education Center

© 2013 Elsie Spittle
www.3phd.net

ISBN: 1484933966
ISBN 13: 9781484933961
Library of Congress Control Number: 2013909462
LCCN Imprint Name: CreateSpace Independent Publishing Platform,
North Charleston, SC

First printed in 2013
Printed in the USA

Editor: Jane Tucker
Author Photo: Rudi Kennard

Note from the Author

This collection of stories is true; in certain chapters relating to business and personal relationships, names and gender have been changed to protect the privacy of those involved. Read slowly, savoring and absorbing each paragraph, so insights have a chance to emerge from your wisdom. It is my wish for you that you hear something new which will inspire and transform.

Contents

Foreword

Imagine you've been blindfolded throughout much of your life; then a friend comes along and with a few mystical words, helps to remove the blindfold. Now, you experience life as never before. Each day brings new learning. You see familiar sights as if you have a new set of eyes. What had been gray is now in full color. You are stronger in your confidence and capabilities. Your outlook is filled with possibilities and dreams. Your life moves forward with this new reality as a foundation, and your journey of discovery continues wherever you are.

We can tell you firsthand that this is Elsie Spittle's story and this book is essentially autobiographical. The "friend" is a man named Sydney Banks. Sydney Banks had an epiphany that showed him the true nature of the human experience. He shared with her what he had seen about the principles of Mind, Consciousness and Thought. This knowledge touched her soul and this is what gave her a new life.

The most powerful thing about this book is the back story. During the early part of her journey, Elsie experienced profound insights that accounted for the dramatic changes in her life. She is eloquent in articulating what she learned during those defining moments.

Elsie was Sydney Banks' first student and the first teacher of the principles, after Syd. We have known her for over thirty years, being among the first mental health professionals to learn directly from Sydney Banks and to share what we learned from him professionally. We find her to be a highly regarded teacher. As we write this foreword, the principles Elsie talks about in her book are being taught throughout the world. If you asked experienced practitioners who they respected most as a teacher of these principles, Elsie Spittle's name would always be mentioned. She has shared this understanding with people in many different settings for years, and has changed many lives.

This is a meaningful book that will touch reader's hearts. It offers hope for a life of unlimited possibilities; a life available to anyone who is ready to access their own inner wisdom.

Dr. George and Linda Pransky,
La Conner, Washington, USA

Acknowledgement

My thanks go to the love of my life, my husband Ken. Not only has he been an integral part of my lifelong commitment to sharing the Three Principles, but it was through Ken that I first met Sydney Banks. For this I will always be very, very grateful.

In addition, I extend my deepest gratitude to an absent mentor, Sydney Banks. Absent in body; but his legacy of the Three Principles lives on.

Lastly, I wish to express my thanks for the privilege of working with so many incredible people who came to this understanding, often times struggling, and then finding their inner reality, where peace and contentment reside.

Introduction

Not in my wildest imagination did I ever think I would meet an Enlightened man. I wasn't even familiar with the word "enlightenment" and knew nothing of its deeper meaning. When I first heard the term, I simply thought, "Ah, enlightened about general things in life; someone who is well educated, cultured and sophisticated."

Beyond my comprehension was the thought that an individual could have a spontaneous epiphany that would reveal three foundational Principles, relevant to all, and that such Principles had the power to transform humanity. Enlightening, indeed. But that's what happened to me and my husband, Ken. We met a man who uncovered the secret to life.

This book tells the story of our journey together.

❧꧁꧂❧

Part One

The Early Days

Deep Feelings and Insight

For those of you who know me, or who have read my previous articles or books, you know I experienced a great deal of resistance to Sydney Banks' message of hope and transformation.

Syd and my husband had worked together in a pulp mill for many years. They knew each other fairly well and considered themselves to be good friends. I met Syd about a year before his life took an extraordinary turn.

Syd, an ordinary working man with limited education, experienced a spontaneous epiphany in 1973, revealing three spiritual Principles: Mind, Consciousness and Thought. This illuminating experience transformed Syd before our very eyes. He was never again the same man he had been before.

In the past, he had been rather insecure and hesitant about life, as were we, so we got along very well. After his enlightenment, his whole persona changed to one of confidence; his presence was imbued with an energy I'd never seen in him before. He told us he had discovered the secret to life; that the Three Principles he had uncovered had the power to change the fields of psychology and psychiatry forever. He said these Principles would help alleviate humanity's suffering like nothing before. He made these statements with the utmost conviction and certainty. It was very, very unnerving to Ken and me.

When I heard Syd say, "*People create experience via Thought,*" that idea evoked fear in me. I backed away from taking responsibility for my unhappiness, truly believing that my misery was caused by external circumstances; we had very little money, my family relationships were poor, and there seemed to be no opportunity for change to occur in my life.

My resistance increased as time went on. I saw Syd blossom, and this disturbed me. His relationship with his wife, Barb (who passed away in 1986), flourished after he had his profound experience. Although she too had some initial resistance, within a short period of time she had an insight that allowed her own wisdom to unfold. From then on, she steadfastly helped Syd on his path of sharing his discovery with the world.

As Syd's relationship with his wife thrived, I watched with jealousy and longing; a dichotomy to be sure. On one hand, I longed for the same depth of love and joy I saw expressed in their relationship; on the other hand, I resented that they had such beautiful feelings, and I didn't.

Yet the feeling of compassion and understanding emanating from Syd filled my heart and offered me comfort. The feeling moved me into peace of mind, a mental space I seldom visited. I wanted more of that deep feeling, but how to get there was a puzzle to me.

Syd always talked about the power of deep feelings. He would say things like, *"Just listen; if you get a beautiful feeling, that's it. That's what you're looking for. That beautiful feeling is where all the answers lie."*

I wanted to believe him, but found it very, very difficult. Nonetheless, in spite of myself and my resistance, I sought out Syd's company so I could feel happy by osmosis. Little did I know that the deep feeling I was experiencing was my inner self being woken up, little by little.

At one point, while I was at my lowest ebb, Syd and Barb arrived at our home for an unplanned visit and knocked on the door. I dreaded their company, yet it was after that brief but significant visit that I had my own watershed moment.

I've told this story many times but I feel it bears repeating in this book. By this time, Syd and Barb had moved from our town of Nanaimo to Salt Spring Island; it had taken them a ferry ride and an hour's drive to get to our home. When I saw them driving up, I couldn't bear the thought of visiting with them because I was feeling so depressed. The world I knew was crumbling around me. Everything I had believed in was now shattering into pieces. I didn't have any solid base to support me and felt my life was over before it had begun.

So agitated was my state of mind when they arrived that I didn't know where to go to avoid answering the door, so I hid in the bathroom. Looking back on it now, the toilet was a most fitting place, in light of the way I was feeling!

I heard Syd's voice announcing their presence in our home and refrained from answering, holding my breath until I heard the door close after their departure. As if an unseen hand pushed me out of the bathroom, I suddenly found myself in the kitchen running after them. I opened the door and beckoned them back in.

As they entered, I stood by the stove thinking I'd make them a cup of tea. I found it impossible to look Syd in the face and busied myself with the kettle. Syd took one look at my distressed expression and with such gentleness and love spoke these words to me: *"You'll be okay, dearie. God is within you and everyone in the world. You'll be okay."* With those words, he put his arm around my shoulders and hugged me. I couldn't stand it. I found myself literally escorting them to the door making some inane comment about having tea another day.

I was so relieved to see them go. What he had said about God being within everyone infuriated me. You'd think those words would have helped me, but instead they were the last straw and inflamed my senses. The final barrier in my mind had been breached. I had nothing left to stand on.

People have asked me why I got so upset with those words Syd spoke to me. I didn't know why for a long time. Ultimately, I realized it was because I questioned his authority and certainty in making such a statement. How could he know such a thing? What gave him the right to tell me that God was within me and everyone in the world?

I'd never heard anyone talk about God like Syd did. I was brought up with a religious background and had believed only priests had the authority to talk like that. And I hadn't been raised to believe God was within me. I had believed God was up in the sky, not of this world, and certainly not a part of humanity. So for Syd to talk so knowledgeably and with such familiarity about God totally destroyed my belief system. To believe that God was within me, feeling as unworthy as I did, was an enormous leap of faith for me to take and I simply couldn't do it at that time.

After Syd and Barb left, I called a mutual friend and related the past hour of my experience. As I raged on and on, my tirade was met with silence. This was a very unusual response. Normally when this friend and I talked about the latest thought provoking thing Syd had said, we were in total accord. This time she said nothing; she just listened. Finally as I wound down, spent with fatigue and stress, she said, "Elsie, you should really listen to yourself. I've never heard you like this."

I felt betrayed and hurt by what I considered her lack of understanding. I thought to myself, 'some friend you turned out to be' and slammed down the phone. In that moment, a glimmer of light pierced my consciousness and I had my first insight. I realized it was my thinking that was creating my resistance. My inner struggle had nothing to do with my circumstances, or with Syd's sharing true knowledge with me. It was me, using the power of Thought against myself, in innocence.

With this realization, my mind felt like it was being cleansed, releasing years of negativity. I found myself filling with gratitude;

my throat tightened with emotion and tears coursed down my face. I'd never felt so energized and at the same time rather vulnerable. My heart felt full of love for Ken and for my children. I couldn't wait for them to come home so I could wrap my arms around them and hold them close to me.

The thought came to me of the enormous patience Syd had shown, in spite of the challenging and disrespectful tone I had sometimes adopted when questioning his philosophy. I was eager to share with him what had happened to me after he and Barb had left.

Once they'd had time to return to Salt Spring Island on the ferry, I called and apologised for my poor behavior, expressing my deepest appreciation for the fact that he had not given up on me. I told him I was beginning to see that something extraordinary must have happened to him, something so out of the realm of the ordinary world we lived in that it felt like a fairy tale to me.

Syd was very moved by my call. *"I knew you heard something today, Elsie. Barb was concerned when we left your home; she thought that was the last time we would see you. But I told her not to worry, that you'd heard something. Barb replied to me, 'She sure has an unusual way of showing it – She basically showed us the door!'"*

Just after I got off the phone, with Syd promising we would talk soon, Ken arrived. We had a while on our own before the kids would be home on the school bus. I related my afternoon's adventure to him and shared my insight. To be honest, he wasn't really impressed. He was still feeling the way I had before; he was ambivalent about Syd's experience and what he shared with us. Like me, Ken really enjoyed Syd and Barb's company as long as Syd didn't talk "truth." Ken considered it was Syd's "truth," and that it didn't necessarily apply to everyone.

It took a bit of time before Ken sensed that the truth Syd was talking about was Universal and that the Three Principles Syd uncovered were foundational: all humans have the ability to create their own experience. Once Ken got a feeling for the universality of Syd's message, he never wavered and always supported Syd in any way he could.

The realization that thought creates feeling gave new meaning to my life. My world opened up in a way I had never imagined possible, leading to a life far beyond any of my early dreams of being a contented wife and mother with an exciting career, and a chance to travel and experience the world beyond my narrow confines.

Syd told Ken and me, not too long after we began to study in earnest with him, that we would travel the world, sharing the message of hope for humanity, telling people of their divine birthright.

The secret that had been revealed to Syd became a gift for all humanity.

Beyond imagination? Most definitely—into a whole new reality.

Learning to Share

Shortly after that turning point in our life, Syd suggested Ken and I share what we were learning about the Principles in our hometown of Nanaimo. Syd saw that Ken and I were both changing, living in more harmony with each other and with our children, so he encouraged us to offer what we had learned, with respect, to those who were genuinely interested. He told us how important this was; that when you do this, you learn more yourself, as well as giving hope and inspiration to others.

How people heard about the Principles was curious – one couple had known Syd before his experience and wondered about his transformation. So we invited them, as well as other friends, and slowly, by word of mouth, people would contact us to find out more.

We had many amusing experiences and, frankly, some not as entertaining, as we offered what little we knew to those who came to the meetings we hosted. At first, we invited friends and colleagues to our home; as the groups got larger, we found small community centers to hold the meetings.

Sometimes Syd would come and talk to the group and of course, those sessions were outstanding. We would see people melt with the warmth and humor he brought to his talks; people we had found difficult to reach, when we were conducting the groups, were having insights in the moment while Syd talked. How he did this was unfathomable to me; I just watched with respect, and in total admiration.

Other times, we did the best we could on our own; sharing our insights and more importantly, sharing the feeling of gratitude for discovering something so essential to understanding the human psyche.

With the Principles being so new to me, there were times when my old ego took hold if I was challenged during a meeting. I would hold firm to make a point, without really listening to the other person.

I remember one fellow saying to me, "You're just into your ego, Elsie."

I responded indignantly and emphatically, "No, I'm not!"

We went back and forth for a few minutes until I realized how silly this was, and that of course I was gripped by my ego when a situation like this occurred, and the feeling became negative. Funny thing; once I stopped persisting in my personal opinion, so did he. . .

I remember a particularly eventful evening. A number of musicians began coming to the group and I invited them to play at the beginning of the meeting, thinking it would relax everyone so the discussion could really get going. Soon there was more music going on in the meetings than conversation. We thought it was great, although I will admit I had a guilty feeling in the pit of my stomach, sensing that all was not right. We were meant to be sharing the wonder of the spiritual power within humanity, rather than the musical talent of a few individuals.

Syd came to one of those meetings and as the musicians enthusiastically continued to play, not providing space for Syd to speak, he raised his eyebrows at me as if to say, "What this about?"

That look silenced the room. In short order, stillness came upon the group and Syd was able to bring about a warm, beautiful feeling as he spoke of the unparalleled qualities of the Three Principles he had uncovered.

We learned a great deal about the importance of keeping the feeling positive during our meetings, and how to listen with respect; especially when someone got stuck in their own thinking and couldn't feel their inner spirit. Those times were the most critical in our early learning, because we saw the power of the deep feeling that is released from within, and how that feeling settles people down so they can hear their own wisdom, and gain insight.

I'm often asked by people who are new to the Three Principles understanding how to share this gift with others. They've had an insight that has changed their lives, and now feel compelled to share what they've found.

Sometimes people get insecure about sharing because of their lack of education, as if formal education has something to do with insight and wisdom. In my mind, when someone has an insight, it's like a diploma; a diploma from the school of innate wisdom.

When we share the gift of the Principles, it is the powerful force of love from within that acts as a catalyst to awaken the dormant self in others. Love promotes the feeling of safety and openness which leads to insight—each person's own insight, which is pertinent to that individual's unique life.

The Three Principles Syd uncovered reveal the knowledge that people have the power and the right to touch the living essence within their own soul. That essence is our birthright, our natural spiritual home. Here is where insights are born; insights that correct our lives, alleviate our suffering, and restore harmony with our spiritual self.

The Nature of Faith

$\mathcal{B}$ack when we were all still living in Nanaimo, Syd and Barb invited us to come over to Salt Spring while they were vacationing there. They had a charming, but small, cottage on the island so they suggested we bring our camper for sleeping. This was the first time Ken and I were asked to stay at the Banks' place so we were quite excited.

Clear blue skies and shining sun welcomed us as we drove into the ferry parking lot in Crofton early one morning. We had arranged to meet Syd at the ferry terminal, where we would travel together to his home. Once we parked our car, we got out to stroll around the waterfront area. We spied Syd down on the pier by a fishing boat and as we walked toward him, we noticed he was munching on something. He grinned at us and handed us some shrimp, saying they had just been cooked and were "the best shrimp" to be had. We proceeded to peel and enjoy our delicious bounty.

Although this trip occurred before Syd had his profound experience, he had a way, even then, of enjoying the simple pleasures in life, beyond what we were accustomed to.

Later, after the spiritual epiphany that transformed his life, we noticed that his ability to just *be*, and to savor each precious moment, was clearly enhanced. So many times, we heard him say something like, *"This is the best fish and chips I've ever tasted,"* or *"This is the best cup of tea,"* or *"That was the best phone call I ever had."* And at that moment in time, you could see that for him, it *was* the best ever. His capacity to experience life to the fullest helped us enjoy the ordinary but special moments of life as well. It seemed everyone Syd came in contact with was drawn to this deep sensitivity and appreciation for what life had to offer. He embodied simple but profound enjoyment at the same time.

Another distinctive feature I observed after his experience was that Syd had the deepest understanding of the spiritual nature of faith, quite beyond the intellect. I remember when he and Barb were planning their move to the island just after he left his job in Nanaimo. Ken and I were concerned that Syd didn't have any employment lined up. We asked what he planned to do to support his family. His answer was simplicity itself: *"Faith is true knowledge being manifested into form."*

Syd told us he *knew* he and his family would be provided for. He *knew* his time had come to serve others by sharing his discovery of the Principles. His faith was unshakeable and illustrated the strength and power of *knowing* from within.

There were times, I know, when things were tight financially for them, yet they never stopped giving to others. Their generosity equaled their faith. They lived the old adage, "To give is to receive."

After Syd and Barb moved to Salt Spring Island, he began in earnest to offer his service to humanity. People were drawn to him as if by a spiritual magnet. Individuals struggling with mental health issues came down his driveway and knocked at his door, saying, "I hear you can help people." Syd was always so kind, and would tell the person that he was not a doctor or psychologist, but they were welcome to come in for a cup of tea. So many incredible transformations took place over a cup of tea.

Ending the Search

*T*here are many memorable times, held dear to my heart, in our journey with Syd. I remember one time in particular, shortly before we moved to the island; Syd had come on his own to visit Ken and me. We lived on a half-acre lot, situated across the road from the picturesque Nanaimo River, in a cozy A-frame home surrounded by giant cedar trees.

Nestled on big, comfy cushions, we sat before our aged cast-iron wood stove, gazing into the glowing flames. Syd began to speak about the wonders of the spiritual world hidden inside each living soul, and of the power and majesty this realm offered to humanity, once it was found.

He spoke with a soft Scottish burr, so sometimes you had to listen carefully to hear him. But this particular evening, it seemed as if his words were coming from inside me, and I was mesmerized by the picture he painted, and the feeling I was experiencing. It seemed like my soul was blossoming, expanding to fill my whole being, and beyond. I knew this feeling must be coming from that spiritual essence that lies within us all; but wondered, "How to keep it?" I had never felt like this before and I cherished the feeling, wanting to preserve it in my heart and soul forever.

Later, as I tried to describe my emotion to Syd, and how I wanted to "save" that feeling, he chuckled and shook his head. I don't recall his exact words, but he said something like this: *"Dearie, you don't have to save that feeling. It's your true self coming* to life. Just enjoy it and you'll find even deeper feelings. If you try and hang on to it, you'll lose it. Just know that you are that feeling, and trust that it's there for you, always."

During that visit, Syd invited us to come and stay for the weekend at their home on Salt Spring Island. He wanted us to meet some of the people who had sought him out, wanting to learn about the mystical gift he had uncovered. We were honored to receive this invitation, and very curious to see what Syd would talk about and how he would present himself.

When we arrived at the Banks' home Saturday evening, I didn't know what to expect. Barb embraced us as we came through the door, welcoming us with such warmth that I immediately felt at ease. We were pointed to the front room, and as I paused in the doorway, I felt my breath taken away. It was a modest room, but it appeared to glow with a special light; I knew this was the room where Syd had had his profound experience. I sensed a quiet, mystical resonance, even though the room was filled with people surrounding Syd, listening attentively as he talked with them.

He looked up and beckoned us over, introducing us to the group. Shortly, I found myself ensconced on the sofa, drinking in the beauty of the room. Honey colored panelling covered the walls, adding a warm, rich tone to the ambiance; the large front room window overlooking the ocean was enhanced with velvet drapes of a deep russet color. On the opposite wall, facing the window was a rustic old stone fireplace that Syd had built himself. The fragrance of the fire added to the atmosphere.

The floor was covered with gorgeous, timeworn Oriental carpets. Comfortable, chintz covered sofas faced each other across the room, and two handsome wingback chairs, one in each corner, completed the furniture arrangement. There were exquisite lamps, with old fashioned shades, that cast a soft light. Here and there, fresh flowers were displayed on various small tables. It was a beautiful room, warm and inviting.

Soon, a hush descended upon the group as Syd took his place, sitting on a cushion on the fireplace hearth, his back resting lightly against the stone. His face looked utterly at peace. The stillness prevailed; then, in his soft Scottish brogue, he began to speak.

Syd's talk carried us all to inner heights and transformed people's faces as if by magic. Gone from their features was any hint of stress that had been visible when we first arrived. Instead, as I looked around the room, I saw people with sparkling eyes, alive with vitality, looking relaxed, healthy and happy. It mirrored what we were feeling, and the way our own earlier anxiety had vanished without a trace.

Syd's talk illustrated the power and depth of his understanding; an understanding that was not of this world, but of an inner dimension. You could feel the presence of pure Consciousness, of pure Mind and pure Thought, being expressed through the form of the man known as Sydney Banks. It was an incredibly inspiring evening, never to be forgotten. Clearly, the spiritual energy manifested in the room that night had the power to change people. It was the beginning of seeing countless individuals, over the years, come alive when introduced to their true nature.

After the evening ended, Ken and I were shown to a tiny cottage located on the same property, next door to their home. Barb's mother, Mary, usually lived in the cottage, but this particular weekend she was away visiting her son and family. It was a comfortable room, finished with cedar panelling, with windows overlooking the ocean so you could hear the sound of the waves. The bed had a lovely down comforter so we snuggled in, cozy as two peas in a pod.

As we lay in bed, chatting about the people we'd met and Syd's talk, Ken commented on how powerful the gathering had been for him. "The feeling was palpable tonight. No wonder Syd talks about how important it is for people to share what they've learned. I could see that as Syd talked, he was moved to greater heights himself. And that feeling, as he went deeper, permeated the room and lifted people's spirits. It certainly lifted mine."

The last thought that came to me, as I felt my eyes begin to close, was how grateful I was to have such a partner as Ken. Travelling this journey with Syd was somewhat of a roller coaster ride, and I was not fond of roller coasters. Yet the ride got gentler as I learned more about my inner resources. To share the learning with Ken, and to see how he was growing, filled my heart. I snuggled closer to him and we drifted off to sleep, content in our cocoon, hearing the ocean in the background, gently lapping at the shore.

The next morning, over a hearty breakfast of sausage and eggs, Ken related to Syd how he had felt about the previous evening. "You know it's been difficult for me to hear you, Syd. All the years we worked together before your experience has been a barrier to my hearing you now. But last night, something happened to me, and I heard you differently than I ever have before."

Syd's faced creased into a huge smile. *"I could see something was happening to you, Ken. It seems to me that you've stopped the search. You are seeing there is something inside yourself that can help you. I'm glad. You're my long-time buddy and it's nice to see you happy."*

Throughout the years of Syd's teaching, he often spoke about the natural elimination of the need to continue searching for answers outside oneself. *"Once you realize, even a little, who and what you truly are, you have no need to search for answers,"* he said. *"The knowledge you seek lies deep within your soul."*

As the years passed, I observed many searchers who came to meet with Syd. Some gained insight that transformed their lives, and the change continues to manifest to this day; others came and left without hearing a word. Then there were those who heard something, yet when their insight seemed to fade they embarked upon another journey, pursuing the latest approach or theory that they thought would help. They continued to look for something outside themselves.

Everyone has a choice to seek inside or outside oneself. In the present time, I find myself moved by the capacity humans have to *know*. I see that when we get a glimmer of our true identity, even when we get lost from time to time, we *know* the answer lies inside. It's just a matter of patience and trust that our level of consciousness will shift to a deeper level of insight once again. This is an amazingly profound and helpful gift.

This gift frees the mind to live in more peace and harmony, not worrying about "getting it." It, true knowledge, is already ours; just waiting to be released and lived in more of the time. All that is necessary is to simply enjoy the inner journey!

The Core Group

One of the things that really impressed us was meeting the small group of people who were the first drawn to listen and learn from Syd. They had such a wonderful, warm and welcoming feeling that you couldn't help but join in their laughter and enjoyment of life.

The other significant point I remember is how attentive that small group was toward Syd. They really listened. They didn't argue or debate. Questions were asked, of course, but when Syd responded, they paid attention. This observation was a novel experience for Ken and me. We were used to disregarding much of what Syd told us—or at least this was how we had acted in the early part of our relationship, before we *heard*. As a matter of fact, more than disregarding, we had outright challenged him, and couldn't understand why he wouldn't get into the challenge with us. His enigmatic look often drove me to distraction. Yet here was this lovely, interesting group of people listening to the man with total attention. It gave me pause, and prompted me to listen as well.

As I began to learn more about this group, I heard that many had chosen to leave society and live an alternative life style know in the seventies as "going back to the land." They felt that society was going down the wrong road. Some of the group were well educated; lawyers, teachers, and so on. Others were from the trades, as Syd had been a welder and Ken, a pipefitter. Carpenters, plumbers, all these varied people were the first drawn to the warmth of Syd's love and message of hope.

As Syd talked with these individuals, he helped them see that they were part of society and if they *heard* his message, they could help change the social order by becoming responsible citizens and sharing their wisdom with the system rather than opting out.

And indeed, as these people gained insight, they did contribute wholeheartedly to the community of Salt Spring and beyond. Lawyers who had left their practices founded new businesses on the island and guided people with heart as well as their legal expertise; construction companies were started and some magnificent homes were built with love and creativity; various other shops and restaurants were opened; teachers helped the schools they were in become more in service to the children, parents, and staff. This new feeling of service, coming from wisdom, eliminated much of the stress the schools had been experiencing.

The re-entry of all these individuals into society was done with grace and dignity; and yes, a lot of hilarity at times at some of the gaffes that were made. Of course there were ups and downs as there would be in any new undertaking. But there was an amazing energy in those early days that defies description. Suffice to say, there was a mystical feeling that seemed to permeate the island because Syd's experience had taken place there. Combined with the new energized industry displayed by the core group, the island took on a new demeanor that drew many from around the world to the beauty and the loving feeling that pervaded the community.

It became quite clear to us that something extraordinary was happening on this little island and we wanted to be a part of it. We realized what a privilege it was to learn from Syd, and knew it was time to move to Salt Spring to be near him and Barb, to continue our inner education.

We relocated to Salt Spring Island about two years after the Banks' had moved there. The example they set by living in faith inspired us immensely. It helped calm us down when we began to worry about the future. In addition, there was such an abundance of learning from Syd that we were enriched, spiritually and psychologically, as our understanding of the true nature of life and of humanity increased.

I remember Syd talking with us and that early, core group of people at his home, describing what life is like when you wake up spiritually and your inner self is revealed.

Syd's eyes were bright with unshed tears as he shook his head in wonder, "*Sometimes since my experience, my life feels like the mystical movie Brigadoon. It feels as if the mists of time have lifted and shown me a whole new world.*"

I found out later that the mythical story of Brigadoon was set in a magic Scottish village which comes out of the Highland mists once every hundred years. . .

Yes, what happened to Syd sounded like a fairy tale to us; and yet the fact remained, the proof was before our very eyes. Countless people began coming to the island from all over the world; gurus from India, self-awareness leaders from Europe and North America, CEO's of major companies, ordinary people looking for help, for a better way to live life. If you asked them how they had heard of Syd, they often told a mystical story of how they arrived on the island.

I remember when a group of human development specialists from Europe arrived on Salt Spring. Syd invited us over to meet with them; we were delighted as these talks always stretched our minds to new depths.

During a moment of casual conversation, I asked how they had heard of Syd. One fellow responded that he had spoken with a colleague in the States, who told him of a rumor about an unusual occurrence that had taken place on an island; an account about an ordinary man who'd had a transcendent experience, and now knew something beyond the realm of the physical world. Their organization wanted to learn more about this. He said it was a "feeling" that prompted them to investigate this extraordinary story.

Another man who came to the island told me he had seen a photo of Syd on a poster at an awareness center in Vancouver, and was struck by the look of serenity on Syd's face. When he asked the staff about it, no one really knew how the poster had gotten there, or who Syd was, but they encouraged the man to go to Salt Spring to meet him. They said Syd looked like a very wise man who could help people.

There are thousands of stories like this. The one thing they all have in common is that the individuals were drawn to Syd by the "feeling;" a feeling that Syd knew something that offered hope and solace to humanity.

There were many who came, but few who really heard. Yet Syd was always patient with those who simply could not grasp the enormity of his discovery. Often times, he commented that he learned more than his guests.

Over the thirty-eight years Ken and I have been on this spiritual journey, we've lived on Salt Spring, moved to Vancouver, then Miami, later on to Tampa, on to Long Beach in California, and finally, full circle, back to Salt Spring. Each time, true faith has guided us from within; most of the time, with barely a penny to our names. We *knew* that we would be taken care of if we were truly in service to humanity, helping as best we could to share this treasure, the gift of the Three Principles.

I've seen this same thing happen with so many others. The core group who first listened to Syd all have lives that challenge the norm, living in faith where opportunities arrive that support and sustain the human spirit. Syd's example continues to motivate and inspire us, and countless others.

A Meeting of the Minds at Vesuvius Beach

Some of my fondest memories of the early years with Sydney Banks occurred at Vesuvius Beach. In the warm days of summer, my family and I would head to the beach to enjoy the simple pleasures of a swim and picnic. Located in the picturesque seaside village of Vesuvius, about ten or fifteen minutes to the northwest of Ganges, there is beach access with stairs leading down from the street above.

The beach is a beautiful cove, with gentle waves lapping at the shore, and a gradual incline to the ocean. We spent many happy hours there, watching our children play in the sea. Our son loved to skim flat stones across the water and often his Dad would join him, seeing who could get the most skips. Our daughter, three years younger, would try her hand at this event, flinging handfuls of pebbles as far as she could, content to be included in the play.

The ferry from Vesuvius to Crofton, on Vancouver Island, offered additional entertainment, as we observed vehicles and passengers land and depart. As bigger waves rolled in with the ferry, the children would sit atop large pieces of driftwood that floated close to shore, picturing them to be surf boards. They would leap up, arms waving wildly, as they precariously balanced on their logs, hoping for a ride. The wood was so water logged it barely floated, but in the children's vivid imaginings, you never knew. You might catch a wave.

Our friends would arrive with their families. All of us had brought picnic baskets, laden with fried chicken, ham, potato salad, and coleslaw, with tasty desserts to finish the meal. Pot luck style was typical, and relished, as everyone got to taste someone else's speciality.

Sometimes Syd and Barb, and now and again, their children, would join us on the beach. This was always a special occasion – although it was an ordinary beach outing, Syd had a way of making the ordinary, extraordinary.

Toward sunset, as the children nestled close to their parents, replete with food and sun, they would sleepily drift off, or quietly listen to their parents' conversations. There were memorable moments when Syd might say a few words about how lucky we all were, to have found this happiness within; a few words that meant the world to all of us, attentive to every nuance of his presence.

I remember him telling us all that time spent with family was one of the most important things we could do in nourishing the innate health of our children. He spoke about the world's children as our future leaders and that if we lived in Truth, our children would pick it up by osmosis. Syd told us that in this way, loving our families and putting them before anything else, including work or career, we were offering hope and sanity to society.

"Don't try and teach your children about the Principles," he said, "Just live with love in your hearts and they will grow into the most beautiful, mentally healthy people you could hope to find, safe for the rest of their lives." He went on to say how that would break the cycle of family dysfunction many of us had experienced in our backgrounds, prior to learning about the Principles.

Syd told Ken and me in the very beginning, shortly after he had his epiphany, that psychologists, psychiatrists, and therapists would seek him out, to find out about the secret to life he had uncovered. How he knew this, I don't know. I just know he was certain it would occur.

Somehow, word began to spread in the psychological community about Syd and the remarkable results he, a non-professional, with only a ninth grade education, was having with troubled souls. Professionals in the field heard that he was successfully helping people who had been struggling with depression and a host of other mental health issues. I imagine that stimulated a lot of conversation. How could an ordinary person, with limited education and knowing nothing about psychology, help persons who had been suffering for years from various traumas?

Amongst the first to arrive were two psychologists, Dr. Roger Mills and Dr. George Pransky, accompanied by George's wife, Linda. They came to investigate this phenomenon. Syd felt they heard something that stirred them deeply, although they didn't have a clue what it was. They began to visit him more often. They were very intrigued, but mystified, by the discussions they had with him. At times, they became frustrated trying to understand the new paradigm Syd was describing. They couldn't pin him down with their traditional logic of looking to change clients' behavior, rather than *seeing* the source of behavior as being created via the Principles.

The other point the professionals found hard to understand was that people are innately mentally healthy. Their training was focused on dysfunction—what was wrong with people—not what was healthy and whole.

During Syd's profound experience that uncovered the Three Principles, he realized, in that timeless moment, that there is no insecurity; insecurity is just a thought. He knew in that instant that people are born with inner wisdom, which, when tapped into, will provide all the answers to life's dilemmas. Furthermore, the inner wisdom continues to guide throughout one's life. This new way of *seeing* humanity was totally opposite to the beliefs traditional psychology held then and, for the most part, continues to hold to this day.

The proof started with the fact that Syd himself underwent a radical behavior change after his spiritual Enlightenment. His behavior, his whole being, was transformed through the insight he'd had into the Three Principles. He didn't have to "work" on his behavior or try to improve; his transformation happened naturally, from the inside out. From that moment on, he *knew* he was taken care of for the rest of his life. He didn't know how, but he knew he would be okay, no matter what.

He also knew his work was cut out for him, that it wouldn't be easy, but that he really had no choice. Given an extraordinary gift of such historic significance, he willingly devoted his life to sharing the gift of true knowledge with others.

Drawing upon the innate wisdom of people, which resulted in positive change, proved it was not only unnecessary to go back to the past to explore the "why's" and "how's" of problems; it was essentially dangerous to do so. Raking up past problems merely reinforced the problems.

The body of proof grew as people learning from Syd began to uncover their own wisdom, experiencing amazing life changes without going into the past. This was, without a doubt, a new paradigm in the mental health field.

I remember Syd, with tongue in cheek, solemnly asking one psychologist why he took his clients back into their past problems to find happiness. As best as I can remember, Syd said, with his gentle charm and a twinkle in his eye, *"Isn't that like asking them to get in a leaky boat in order to get to shore?"* The man was rather nonplused by this statement, but to his credit, he continued to listen to Syd, albeit with a little more attention.

Syd had such a genius for helping people relax and experience the joy of ordinary, day to day life. The two psychologists mentioned earlier, George Pransky and Roger Mills became increasingly impressed by the new paradigm Syd had discovered and wanted to spend more time studying with him. Syd was delighted in their interest because he knew that as George and Roger changed they would be able to help their clients more. He also foresaw that these two psychologists could have great impact on the mental health field.

George and Roger decided to bring their families to Salt Spring for the summer. They were touched by the relaxed, convivial atmosphere they observed amongst the families and friends close to Syd. They, too, longed for a better quality family life, and wanted to be part of the island community surrounding Syd.

One day, the newcomers, with their children, were invited by Syd to join us all at the beach. Coming down the stairs toward the seaside, I could see by their faces they were a little nervous at meeting us all in such a casual setting. Most of us had met them before at various talks Syd had given on the island, but this was the first informal gathering with all our families together.

Before long, they started to ask us some questions about how our lives had changed since we'd been learning about the Principles. When we shared our "before" and "after" stories, describing the stress in our family lives before we discovered how our thoughts created our stress, they found it difficult to believe. The "after" picture they saw was considerably different from the "before" picture we had painted. They told us they saw calm, confident, mentally healthy people; happy people. That happiness is what they wanted to investigate, not only for their clients, but for themselves and their families.

Recalling some of the early stories of how serious we had been in the past, diligently trying to find happiness, brought great hilarity to the group. We all had a wonderful time, full of warmth and camaraderie, and the enjoyment of getting to know one another; seeing beyond the image of who we each thought the other was, just seeing each other as people, parents and families.

I think it was an eye-opening event for all of us. I know it certainly was for me, as I'd always had some insecurity about being a non-professional meeting a professional. In my mind, that day at the beach brought the understanding that underneath our various disguises, we are all the same spiritual energy; it levelled the playing field from that time forward. It was a meeting of the minds in the truest sense.

Living "Inside"

One of the first things Syd shared with Ken and me, after he told us of his experience, was about going "inside." The phrase baffled us. What could going "inside" possibly mean? I, personally, had enough trouble trying to live in the world around me, and I know Ken felt the same. How could one go "inside"? What was the benefit? Was it even possible? Ken wondered, "Where's the door?"

Of course we peppered Syd with these questions. To our chagrin, he would respond with a twinkle in his eye, saying, *"Just listen; listen for a feeling; quieten your mind, and you will see."*

His response was rather disappointing to us. We considered ourselves pragmatists and wanted concrete answers, but we felt he refused to give them to us. In hindsight, months later, I *saw* that he had given us the answer. We just hadn't *heard* him. It is only when you slip into the experience of "inside" that you know the benefits, and realize that "inside" is, indeed, reality. Furthermore, it is our birthright, our heritage, to live there as much as possible.

Part of our journey is learning about the naturalness of going inside, finding solace in the spiritual essence at our core; then re-joining the outer world, filled with more understanding. This innate wisdom is our guide, always by our side, through stormy weather or blue skies.

Of course, there are countless times we lose sight of this spiritual fact. Over time, as we miss the feeling and the comfort that wisdom offers, we realize that going "inside" is what prompts more learning and continued inner evolution.

I remember the first time I spoke publicly, at Syd Banks' request, to a group of mental health professionals who had invited him to give a seminar on the Three Principles. When he asked me to accompany him as a guest speaker, I was honored and also afraid. While I was in his presence, I felt safe. The moment I was on my own, heading to the auditorium to speak with this group, I became terrified. Even though I was escorted and introduced by Drs. Mills and Pransky, I felt paralyzed by fear.

However, the moment I shared my story of the first time I engaged my true self, "inside," calmness came over me. I remember, as if it were yesterday, the words that came out of my mouth, without volition: "I found a way to be happy." Out of that deep feeling of peace within, true knowledge came to the forefront, and seemed to touch not only me, but my audience as well. The stillness that was felt by all, at the end of my short talk, held us captive for a timeless period. That was the first presentation I gave where I realized it wasn't me talking; it was my true self. This realization gave me a new sense of confidence, of comfort; knowing that I wasn't on my own, that I had wisdom holding my hand.

Later, when I described to Syd how calmness came over me, despite the feeling of fear that had held me paralyzed for a few moments, he said, "*I knew your talk would go well.*" I was taken aback by his certainty. I definitely had not felt that; quite the opposite, as a matter of fact. He told me that whenever we get out of our own way, our inner wisdom is always there to guide us. "*When you go inside, the answers will come to you. That's what happened to you when you had your insight about your thoughts creating your feelings. That's when you discovered happiness.*"

He went on to tell me how it's the same for everyone. Once people realize they are the creator of their own reality, they gain more spiritual power, and their life begins to transform.

An experience I'll never forget regarding going "inside" is the time Syd was invited to talk at a retreat, already in progress, hosted by a group of psychologists who had been learning about the Principles. Evidently, the event was not going as well as they had hoped, and they felt this might be an opportune time to solicit Syd's help. They showed great courage in having Syd come to this mountain retreat to introduce the new paradigm, as they had many other professionals and colleagues in attendance, as well as clients. Syd invited me along, to further my training, and I was humbled as well as excited at the opportunity to learn.

After leaving Salt Spring on a tiny four-seater plane that felt like a Volkswagen with wings, we transferred, in a nearby city, to a larger plane that delivered us closer to our destination. Then we rented a car to travel another couple of hours further into the mountains, where the retreat was held.

Syd was eager to get there and see what awaited us, so we didn't linger on the road but drove straight through. Nonetheless, it felt like an adventure, travelling with Syd, through a rather desolate, uninhabited region until we arrived at our journey's end.

The scene that greeted us impressed itself upon my memory forever more. It was early spring, a cold and cloudy day, with a light mist in the air. In the center of a clearing, surrounded by pine, cedar and other evergreen trees, a few people were gathered around a smoking bonfire, barely burning because of the dampness. Benches made of old logs were scattered here and there, with folks resting upon them. Small cabins were nestled in amongst the forest with a larger community room and kitchen off to the side.

The leader of the group, who had invited Syd to join the retreat, welcomed us both and began to make introductions. Soon we branched off on our own, Syd talking with a few, and

I finding others to chat with. There was a rustle to the side of the clearing and about a dozen more people emerged from the bush. They were shivering with cold, wet to the bone, and looking quite miserable.

They told us they had been white water rafting. None looked like they had enjoyed themselves and when we asked them, they indicated that the weather had not been particularly helpful to their water escapade. Some had fallen into the rapids, been pulled out with great difficulty, and all in all, their adventure had been rather disastrous. For some of the group, their goal had been trying to prove to themselves that they could face their fear of the rapids. Now they were berating themselves for failing to conquer their fear.

Syd took one look at their bedraggled faces, heard their comments about conquering fear and didn't respond. Instead, he busied himself perking up the bonfire. With a few pieces of dry wood and a magic touch, the fire was soon blazing. People gathered around, warming hands and feet; wet clothes were steaming from the heat, and shortly, mugs of hot chocolate and other drinks were making the rounds.

A peace descended upon the group as we sat quietly, entranced by the flames and sparks shooting from the fire. Syd spoke a few words about the upcoming gathering that evening. He mentioned how pleased he was to be there and how much he respected the strength of character of the psychologists who had invited him to attend and to share the Principles he had uncovered. Then he suggested everyone retire to their cabins to get into warm clothes and rest after all their hard work on the river.

"I'll see you later this evening," he said, "and we'll see how to go 'inside' to where your wisdom resides and where fear is recognized for what it really is - thought. There's no need to prove yourself; all you require is some understanding of the true nature of the Principles."

The head psychologist asked if he could meet with both of us for a few minutes before we headed for our respective cabins. Syd acquiesced and we found a quiet spot in the corner of the community center, where the psychologist let us know there were more professionals due to arrive late that afternoon; Gestalt leaders from Europe, we were told.

Syd said, *"That's very interesting."*

The psychologist went on to say, "Some of these Gestalt leaders can be confrontational and very analytical. I just want you to know this before you start your talk, Syd."

Syd looked absolutely calm and unruffled at this news. I could see that our host appeared rather nervous and uneasy. I, myself, was definitely feeling insecure, but I thought, "Syd can handle anything."

Syd looked at me, then at our host, and said, *"I think it would be good if you two started off the talk; share what you've learned, and then you can introduce me."*

The psychologist and I both looked at each other as we agreed, and then quickly looked away. I was there to learn, but I hadn't anticipated speaking before possibly hostile Gestalt trainers. I hurriedly made my excuses and left to find respite in my cabin. My mind was filled with anxiety. Would the trainers attack me verbally? Would they confront my limited knowledge of the Principles? At that moment, I felt I knew nothing of value to offer the group. I was going through my own mental white rapids.

Once in my cabin, my mind calmed down somewhat, and I fell into a restless sleep. Too soon, it was time to head for the community center to have a bite to eat before the talk; but when I got there I couldn't eat a thing.

I saw Syd was surrounded by people, listening attentively to every word. He motioned me over and asked how I was doing. I told him I was terribly nervous about talking. He gazed at me with compassion. *"You're thinking too much. Go 'inside,' share your story and you'll be fine."*

The moment came when my co-presenter and I took the stage. I'd like to say that all at once, I felt calm. Unfortunately, I didn't. Still mired in my little mind, caught up in my fear of the Gestalt people and trying to think of what to say, I could barely talk. My partner clearly felt the same; we quickly introduced Syd and sat down with the rest of the audience.

I waited with bated breath for Syd to begin his talk. I was filled with anxiety for him that he might be confronted by these trainers. Certainly, I had witnessed Syd being attacked verbally before, particularly during the early talks he gave, when what he was talking about was so beyond the understanding of humanity that some would lash out in confusion and fear.

Still, this occasion presented something totally beyond my experience, and I had no idea what would happen. To this day, when I think about that evening, I get chills up my spine and my heart fills to bursting. The moment Syd began to speak, a stillness swept over the room; a presence of such spiritual power was felt that it defies description. In that peace, I found my way inside; I found my way home, and I wept.

A timeless time passed and then Syd was finished. Not a peep was heard. There was a hush as the silence continued. Then people gradually started to leave the hall without a word; couples holding hands, faces utterly at peace, some in tears, as I was.

My co-presenter and I went to Syd as he came down from the stage. His face was glowing with an unutterable light. *"I think everyone seemed to enjoy the talk, didn't they?" he said. "What a nice group they were. I loved seeing the couples leave the hall holding hands. Well, see you tomorrow for breakfast."* And off he went to his cottage.

My friend and I were rendered speechless with that deep mystical feeling and left for our rooms, to cherish the peace within. All the anxiety I had filled my mind with was vanquished by going "inside."

The next morning, the breakfast room was buzzing with energy; cheerful faces greeted one another. I couldn't distinguish the dreaded Gestalt people from any other friendly face. Many told me how deeply Syd's talk had touched them. I honestly don't remember what Syd spoke about. I only know he spoke about the spiritual realm right from the moment he started.

Before we left, later that day, one Gestalt trainer said, "Syd's given me something I've spent my whole life looking for—peace. I couldn't imagine it was possible to feel this way. I was trained to confront and examine every aspect of one's thinking. I would probe into my clients' psyches until they were in pain. I thought this was the way to release their pain. I didn't know that I was innocently creating more suffering. Now I see the answer is right inside us, just waiting to be released, and that people can be healed from the inside-out. There is a simplicity and power to these Principles that I've never experienced before."

I could *see* that Syd had taken us all to a new world; a world within that is filled with peace, true knowledge, and joy.

Learning the Hard Way

*N*ot all my early training experiences were as appreciated by me as the last couple of examples. I remember an incident in San Francisco that gave me pause for quite a long time.

Syd had been invited to give a seminar in the Bay area by Drs. Mills and Pransky. Once again, he invited me to travel with him to the meeting. The morning after we arrived, Syd asked me to welcome the audience and share my story. He suggested Roger join me on stage, which delighted both Roger and me. Syd would arrive later.

I remember talking to the audience about the quality of love, and how I was seeing a new, deeper meaning of the word. For much of my life, my "love" had been quite limited and very conditional; I had expected my family and friends to adhere to a rather rigid standard before I gave my love. I described to the group how my feeling for family and for the world was much more unconditional than it used to be, prior to gaining some understanding of the inner spiritual connection between all things.

Roger supported this theme and contributed his personal experiences. As I began to talk again, building on something Roger had said, a man stood up in the audience and in a loud voice, said, "I wish you would shut up and stop talking about love." Several of his colleagues applauded this statement. The rest of the audience was looking at one another in shock and dismay.

I was frozen for a moment, not knowing what to do. The feeling in the room had been beautiful, warm and welcoming. All of a sudden, with this rude and challenging comment, the feeling plummeted to the floor. I was devastated. Then, without thought, came this statement from within me. "Is this the feeling you want?" I asked the audience, with a quiver in my voice.

With that, I walked off the stage, leaving Roger behind, trying to resolve the situation. I opened the venue door and sped down the hall, tears running down my face. I felt so hurt and humiliated. How could that man say something so hurtful when I was talking about the beautiful feeling of love?

As I careened down the hall, I saw Syd walking toward me. He took one look at me and said, "What happened, dearie?"

As I breathlessly related the story, his eyes twinkled, and he chuckled. I didn't understand his humor and thought it wasn't very kind. My ego was so engaged in what had happened that I didn't realize he was trying to lighten the feeling. He put his arm around my shoulder, gave it a comforting pat, and walked me down the rest of the hallway. "Just forget about it," he said sympathetically. "Let's go have lunch. When I talk to the group this afternoon, I'll fix things. Don't you worry; I'll take care of it." And with that, Roger joined us and we went to lunch.

Food tasted like dust; I couldn't eat. I was regaining some semblance of balance and moving into the feeling of retaliation; remembering Syd's words of, 'I'll fix things,' I envisioned Syd going into the seminar that afternoon, rolling up his sleeves, and giving the man and his cohorts their just desserts! I admit I relished this thought. My understanding was deeply hidden beneath my dark clouds of negative thinking.

Over lunch, someone told us that the man who had confronted me was a well-known author of a series of books about, guess what? – Love!

When we walked into the meeting venue after lunch, Syd took the stage and I sat in the audience. He began to speak; he spoke of the unconditional quality of true love, that this quality had no barriers, no limits, and no judgement. He said that this Divine love was beyond time, space, and matter.

I was shaken by his words. His spiritual presence was so strong that the room felt like we were all enveloped in a cocoon. Not a word, not a challenge was issued from the man who had attacked me. I honestly hadn't expected that he would return and yet, there he was, silenced by Syd's depth of feeling and the truth of his words.

I was taken aback by how Syd handled the situation; he had taken the high road, not the personal road that I projected in my mind. His words had healed the audience from the unpleasant scene that had taken place in the morning.

My mind was still awash with embarrassment for what had happened to me. I couldn't step out of the swamp of my negative thinking. All the talks I'd given prior to this fiasco had been received with respect and with love. What had happened? Was it me? Had I lost the power and feeling of wisdom? Would it ever come back?

That night George, Linda, and Roger invited Syd and me out to dinner. Clytee, a psychiatric nurse who was very interested in the Three Principles, accompanied us. (She later married Dr. Mills) I really hadn't wanted to go to dinner. Staying behind and licking my wounds appealed to me more than dinner with everyone. But Syd encouraged me to join the group and basically said to stop moping.

"Elsie, believe me; this will never happen to you again," he assured me. "You'll learn a lot from this experience. You'll know how to handle this type of thing, should it ever arise again. Now come on, and let your negative thoughts go."

Sitting beside Clytee in the back of a large van on the way to dinner, she made a comment that gave me some solace. She said, "Elsie, I learned so much from what happened this morning; in a way, more than I've learned when the sessions have been really high. When the man censured you and the feeling went down, you said to the audience, 'Is this the feeling you want?' I *heard* that, Elsie. I *heard* that in a way I never had before. I realized I have a choice in the feeling I want to live in. I didn't realize that fully before. Thank you!"

Clearly, Clytee had gained more from the experience than I had. I felt a bit of peace from the truth of her insight but it took a couple of weeks or so before I regained some of my equilibrium. It occurred to me that despite being taken aback by the man's comment, my wisdom had still been available, issuing the sentence to the audience, "Is this the feeling you want?"

Syd shared the story of what happened to me during a talk he gave to the core group on the island, once we returned home. He told it with love, saying how pleased he was with what Roger and I had accomplished in San Francisco. At that point, although I was feeling much more at peace with what had transpired, I really didn't understand what Syd meant by saying Roger and I had accomplished something.

However, I will say that as time went on and I continued my public speaking, I never did experience a situation like that time in San Francisco. Occasionally, there were a few challenges from the audience, but I was able to listen from my wisdom and not from my ego. Then the questions took on an entirely different feeling for me. I began to love questions because it helped me go deeper and come up with answers I'd never realized before.

In some cases, if the challenge was very strong, I realized that the person was, in all probability, experiencing some mental suffering, and simply lashing out from that pain. I didn't take it personally; my heart went out to whoever spoke out. I'd ask the individual to help me better understand the question, and have a dialogue until we felt a degree of alignment. Or, if necessary, I'd suggest we discuss the question or comment during the break.

As time went on, challenging encounters during my presentations simply stopped. I discovered that the deeper you go inside, the more protection wisdom offers you and your audience. When the audience is touched by that deep feeling that arises when we go "inside," most questions are answered "inside" themselves.

I also learned from the San Francisco experience that it didn't serve me well to keep intellectually analyzing "why" that situation occurred. It happened, period. As my mind settled down, wisdom emerged once again, giving me the information I needed to help guide my life.

Syd always cautioned us to "talk what you know." I realized that in that specific situation, I was talking above myself and got into trouble. At that phase of my learning, I really didn't understand the 'spiritual connection between all things' I had spoken about. If I had, I wouldn't have reacted so strongly to the disapproval of the man in the audience. I would have seen beyond his hurt and spoken to the inner core. That's what Syd did, and it healed the hurt.

It was a lesson I needed to learn, through an experience life provided for me. Continuing education! Syd's observation that Roger and I had accomplished something in the Bay area was really about an inner accomplishment. A shift in one's level of consciousness is a spiritual accomplishment, and very welcomed, indeed.

Many years later, someone came up to me at a Principles conference I was attending. He introduced himself to me and asked if I remembered him. I shook my head "no."

He said, "I'm the man who confronted you all those years ago in San Francisco. I've regretted that outburst all these years, Elsie, and I want to apologize. I learned so much from that experience. It changed my life. When I write about love now, it's from a completely different perspective."

Feeling very pleased to have met this man again and seeing how that experience had helped him, I let him know it had been a turning point for me as well. I thanked him; we embraced and went our separate ways, kindred spirits in the journey of spiritual evolution.

On The Job Training

*A*fter Syd's extraordinary experience, he stayed on for ten more months at the pulp mill where he and Ken had worked for many years. However, his relationships with management and co-workers completely changed. Before his experience, Syd would talk with Ken about feeling underutilized at work; he felt passed over for more responsibility, even though he was considered a top tradesman. Consequently, he didn't always enjoy his job. He felt put upon, as did Ken. I remember them discussing this occasionally when we would all get together socially.

This all changed for Syd when he returned to the mill after his insight. He didn't try to change his behavior or the way he saw his work. It happened naturally. Syd was a totally different person with an entirely different perspective. He had compassion for his supervisors, managers, and for his work mates. They began to seek him out to discuss not only work issues, but personal issues as well.

One such person was the plant manager, who invited Syd to his office. Syd was very humbled by the invitation, feeling honored by the manager's request. He never divulged what they conversed about, but it left a lasting impression on Syd that such an invitation should be extended to him. And I'm sure the conversation must have left an equal impact on the plant manager.

About three years later, when we were all living on Salt Spring Island, Syd was invited to the home office of the company that owned the mill, in Vancouver. The vice-president of the division, (we'll call him Glen), had called Syd to see if he would be willing to come over and talk to them about human relations.

Enquiring if I'd be interested in accompanying him, Syd explained to me he felt this trip would broaden my education. Up to this point, I had spoken numerous times on the island and at several universities in the United States, but I'd not had much to do with the corporate world. This trip proved to be one of the most fascinating I had ever taken with Syd.

We arranged our travel, and a week later headed for the Long Harbour ferry to go to Tsawwassen; from there we drove to downtown Vancouver, where the corporate office was located. Before we went, I asked Syd if there was anything I should do to prepare myself. He chuckled, *"Just be yourself, Elsie. I don't know what I'm going to do either. We'll just get together with whoever is there and see what happens."*

Our time on the ferry was uneventful, other than feeling like we were on holiday. We were grinning from ear to ear at the novelty of the situation. *"Did you ever, in your wildest imagination, Elsie, think you and I would be going to the home office of the company Ken and I worked for?"* Syd asked. Equally mystified at how this could be happening, I just shook my head in wonder.

We arrived at our destination, a rather forbidding cement block building with small windows. After finding a parking spot, we took the elevator to the top floor. The receptionist greeted us, saying, "You must be Mr. Banks." Syd nodded and smiled. "They're waiting for you in the board room. Please follow me."

The executive rose from his chair and extended his hand, saying how pleased he was that Syd was able to come to Vancouver. "I've enjoyed speaking with you on the phone and I'm delighted to meet you in person." There was one other man at the table, (we'll call him Mark), who was head of human resources; after introductions were made, we took our seats.

It seemed to me both men were rather nervous and stressed. Their faces were drawn and pale; one of them kept tapping his pen on the table; the other was fiddling with the papers in front of him. Syd seemed not to notice, and began a casual conversation.

Presently, he asked Glen how he could be of service. The executive explained they needed some team work development and hoped Syd could help them. "We've heard you have a unique philosophy that looks at the potential in people, and that you know how to draw it out, to make better leaders who can help motivate and bring out the best in their people. This is what we need; leaders and team members who will take the initiative and ownership of what they do."

Syd listened attentively, nodding his head, and held his silence for a moment. Then he looked at each of the men in turn, and said, *"I suggest we take some time out in the fresh air to consider your request. Are you free for the day?"*

Glen said, "I've booked the whole day off, Syd. We can do whatever you want."

With that, we left the building. Syd recommended we go to Stanley Park, which was located not too far from the office. We all piled into Glen's car and off we went. Syd pointed out a pavilion tucked into a grove of trees, and Glen pulled into the parking lot. As we emerged from the car, we began strolling down the pathway. Syd stopped, bought some peanuts from a nearby vendor, and began to feed the squirrels.

I was rather taken aback by this, although I did find it endearing. Syd was just being himself. Somehow, I had expected he would be more "professional." However, the men seemed to be enjoying our walk, and as Syd passed them the bag of nuts, they too began to feed the squirrels.

Proposing we separate for a while and then meet back at the café in the pavilion for lunch, Syd ambled off with Glen, and

Mark and I went in the opposite direction. Mark commented he was getting a kick out of being away from the office. "I feel like I'm playing hooky from school," he said with glee. I heard this with astonishment. Here I was concerned about Syd being professional, and yet Mark was having a great time. He was definitely looking more relaxed, younger, and his face had gained some color.

After that remark, I too began to relax; we carried on with our walk and casual conversation. Soon Mark began to question me about what I had learned from Syd, and if it was helpful. We had an amazing dialogue; nothing about business, more about family relationships, and about a better understanding of who we are on the "inside." Mark was absorbing all this as if he were a sponge. He thanked me for sharing my stories, and I thought how lucky I was to have this opportunity.

We began to wander back to the café. As we drew near, we could see Syd and Glen in intense conversation, heads together, totally connected. We hesitated for a time, until Syd became aware of us, and beckoned us toward them. They both were beaming. Glen put his arm around Syd's shoulder and said, "Syd, I don't understand what happened to you—but I sure like what you're saying. I'd like some of the confidence you have."

Escorted to a table in the restaurant, we had a delicious lunch, and more fascinating conversation. I don't remember much about the discussion, other than Syd making it clear that the best leaders are those who understand there is no insecurity; only the thought of insecurity. He emphasized that insecurity can vanish in an instant, if you *see* it. He said if the team leader could help his group understand this, the team would succeed beyond what they thought possible. Both Glen and Mark were nodding in agreement. My mind was so full by this time that I really couldn't absorb anymore.

Soon it was time to drive back to the office. Assisting me out of the car, Glen embraced me as he thanked me for joining Syd on the visit. Both men hugged Syd and thanked him profusely for making the trip to Vancouver. Glen said this was one of the best days of his life; Mark agreed it was a memorable day for him as well. They appeared light-hearted as they walked back into the office building with a spring in their step.

How wonderful this is, I thought to myself. Syd Banks has worked his magic once again. We met two stressed, anxious executives this morning. This afternoon, we had left two exuberant, wiser leaders, armed with new insights about personal and professional relationships. They would help their teams develop, no doubt.

With this experience, I learned a great deal about the power of rapport in developing trust, and in building strong relationships. I observed Syd bypass the "executive" disguise presented to us, and I saw him talk to their inner core, where we are all spiritually linked. I saw the impact on these two men as they connected at a deeper level to who they are "inside."

Being taken out of their everyday work environment had been a departure from the usual company culture. That short visit to the park helped them relax, enhancing their listening and allowing their wisdom to surface.

Syd intuitively knew what was needed to be of service to these two leaders, and how this would impact the company as a whole. I had questioned Syd's professionalism—and observed a natural, professional competence that far surpassed anything I had witnessed before.

I didn't know it then, but the insights I gained at this watershed event became, along with the Principles, the foundation for all my future work; whether in business, mental health, urban communities, or juvenile justice. *Seeing* beyond the "disguise" presented—executive, employee, psychologist, counselor, officer, youth, and so on—I learned to speak to the inner core; where we are all the same, and where rapport and connection are made.

Transitions

*W*e lived on the island for four and a half years—a short time in terms of years – but a lifetime in learning. To try and describe all the amazing events that happened on Salt Spring while we were there would be impossible. Suffice it to say that a myriad of people came to the island to learn from Syd. Mysteriously, the island became a magnet for those looking for something deeper and more meaningful in their lives. Some stayed to live and study with Syd, and others came and went.

At one point, Syd began to encourage the core group to consider leaving the island, to strengthen their independence and continue their own journeys out in the world. His life was devoted to helping others, but he also was totally dedicated to his family. He saw that the comings and goings of so many people, including uninvited visitors sometimes just appearing on his doorstep, left no privacy for his family. There were occasions when he would awaken in the morning to discover strangers milling about on his lawn, waiting for Syd to come to the door.

It wasn't the core group that was the issue; this group was very respectful, for the most part, of Syd's time. It was the combination of the multitudes of visitors and friends that prompted those close to him to realize it was, indeed, time to move from the island. Gradually, the core group began to disperse, finding jobs in nearby cities, and in some cases, in other countries.

Of those exiting the island, Ken and I were the last couple to leave. Ken had been working in Vancouver prior to our departure. We had gone through a difficult period in our marriage and had separated for six months. We came back together to save our marriage, and after much consideration, knew it was time for us to seek our good fortune elsewhere.

I'll never forget sitting in the front seat of the moving van we had rented, piled high with furniture, with our two kids tucked in between us, heading for the ferry. My heart felt as if it were breaking. I felt we were leaving the precious "nest" of wisdom Syd had helped nurture; I wondered if I'd ever experience such depth of learning again.

I knew this time on the island had been extraordinary for all of us, including Syd. It was the incubation period, preparing us for sharing what we could of the Three Principles he had uncovered. As I mentioned before, Syd had told Ken and me that if we *heard* him, we would travel the world and share his transcendent message of hope and transformation. I didn't think it would be so difficult to leave and start the journey.

After we had settled in our new home in the Vancouver region, our lives continued in a routine manner. Our children were enrolled in their respective schools. We added some personal touches to our living quarters which helped us feel more at home. Getting together with some of our dear friends, who had moved over earlier, brightened our lives as well. The crowning touch was when Syd and Barb came to visit us and their other friends, putting to rest the picture I'd envisioned of being deprived of Syd's company.

As my life calmed down, I began to feel something stirring deep within my soul. I wanted to share what I had learned, but wasn't sure how to go about it. Then inspiration came.

Approaching community colleges to see if they'd be interested in innate mental health courses, based on the Three Principles, appealed to me. I felt sure the Continuing Education department would be intrigued by this new understanding. I didn't have a degree in psychology; I had been the first in my family to graduate high school and had no further formal education, so I felt a community college would be more flexible and open to my offer than a university, given my limited education.

I began to reach out to other avenues as well; hospitals, businesses, community organizations, but no one seemed attracted to the new paradigm. The Principles understanding apparently was too far removed from the traditional focus of looking at dysfunction in people rather than mental health.

Syd suggested I talk with Chip Chipman to see if we might join forces and do something together. Chip and Jan had been dear friends for a long time while we were all living on the island, and we had gotten together with them again when we moved over to Vancouver.

Chip was working for a manufacturing facility at the time and invited me to visit the site and have a tour. The idea of meeting professionally with Chip was exciting to me. I had a great deal of respect for his business acumen as well as his wisdom. To make a long story short, we ended up starting a business together to provide Principle based training programs. Despite a great many "cold calls," we didn't find any interest for these programs in our regional district, but ultimately both Chip and I were offered jobs in Florida.

An educational institute and clinic was founded in Miami in the early 1980's by a group of psychologists who had studied with Syd. As with the core group, Syd had encouraged these psychologists to share what they had learned with their clients, colleagues, and the mental health profession in general. He knew they had to find a way past the traditional formulations that were the norm, and introduce the field to a completely new orientation toward innate mental health. Syd knew this wasn't going to be easy, but he strongly supported their efforts to take their place as the leaders of this new, innovative paradigm.

I was invited to take a part-time position in this first institute in Miami; Chip joined the group later. Providing leadership training for a mid-sized corporation based in Tampa afforded Chip a wonderful entry into the corporate world. It was the first business organization to introduce the Principles to their company. I was to join him for the second phase of training. We discussed this amazing opportunity with our spouses and all of us agreed, without doubt, this was a chance of a life time.

With glee and anticipation, Ken and I packed a few of our treasured belongings in suitcases and headed, with our daughter, Lynn, for Miami, Florida. Our son, Ron, was already living on his own by then, so he stayed in Vancouver. Chip had left earlier to start training for the corporation, while his wife, Jan, wrapped up things at home and arranged travel for her and their two children to meet him in Miami, where they were going to live. Ken and I were delighted to be making the move with the Chipmans. A new adventure was in store for all of us.

We all lived in Miami for the next year and a half. We helped to organize the clinic, did some training for various groups, and generally made ourselves useful. It was an exhilarating time; a completely different environment that we loved, as well as the opportunity for meeting so many new people who were drawn to the Principles work. Seeing the impact on those who utilized the services of the clinic added to our faith. These simple, powerful Principles were succeeding far beyond our expectations in helping alleviate the suffering of so many in need.

Many times Syd came to Miami to talk at the clinic, and to meet other mental health professionals, as well as physicians and nurses, who were drawn to the exciting results occurring. Syd spoke at the local university and several other venues. He was thrilled to see how his message was giving hope to so many who had considered their lives at an end.

I remember Syd talking with paraplegics and other patients from the Veterans' Hospital in Miami, who had been brought to a seminar he was giving. Included in their treatment program were Principles counseling sessions, so they were familiar with the material, and many had gained significant insights. They were humbled at the opportunity to meet Syd, and to be able to share their amazing stories with the man who had uncovered the Principles–a precious gift that had proved invaluable to them.

I recall one quadriplegic telling Syd he was grateful to have lost the use of his arms and legs, because it gave him the occasion to meet Syd, and to learn about the inner spiritual reality. The patient told Syd how gaining some understanding of who he was on the "inside" had totally altered his perspective of life. Previously, he had felt his life was over, and was filled with despair. Now, despite his physical challenge, he felt his life was enriched with purpose. He wanted nothing more than to help others who were in a similar medical position as he. I recall Syd's eyes filled with tears at this story, and it brought a lump to my throat as well.

The Adventure Continues

$\mathcal{A}$s our involvement increased at the corporation where Chip and I were working, the late Reese Coppage, who was CEO, suggested we move to Tampa. He indicated it would be more cost and time effective than flying back and forth from Miami on a regular basis. We concurred, packed our bags once more, and with families in tow, headed off to Tampa.

Reese was a steadfast supporter of the Principles work. He'd had significant personal insights, and felt there was something very profound in what Syd had experienced. With enormous faith, and a vision for the potential impact of this understanding on his organization, he invited Chip and me to develop a program for his whole company.

After interviewing a cross-section of management and employees, we prepared a report outlining our findings, and provided a training program. We started with one facility, which had requested our services, and eventually worked our way through home office, and the other divisions of the company.

One of the key elements in our decision to interview employees at all levels of the organization was Syd's recommendation at the beginning of our work with business. He was adamant on the importance of gathering information, from the ground floor to top management. In his work at the pulp mill, various consultants had come into the plant and primarily interviewed supervisors and managers. Seldom did they talk with employees who actually did the physical work. Consequently, many of their ideas, when implemented, didn't work well because they didn't recognize the needs of the workers.

This advice was an enormous help to us as we worked with different companies. Gathering a more complete picture of the organization as a whole provided a systemic view, helping us develop relevant training programs. In essence, the training addressed the needs of the overall organization, as reflected in the interviews; as opposed to the views of a specific level of management.

The workers appreciated this attention to detail, and respected Reese for taking the time and spending the financial resources to fund these interviews and trainings. They began to see beyond the "CEO" image they had of Reese, and felt far more comfortable in communicating openly and honestly with him. This pleased Reese, not only as the head of the company, but also as an individual; it was beneficial for him to see the employees in a new light.

I remember one supervisor who, after seeking Reese out in his office, came away delighted at their conversation. "He's so easy to talk to; not at all like I thought. I can see I had a lot of unnecessary thinking going on that got in the way of open dialogue, and sharing creative ideas and solutions."

The increased level of trust, rapport, and communication throughout the company improved not only the human relations climate, but added directly to the profitability of the organization. Workers' compensation and sick leave were reduced as employee stress decreased— just to mention a couple of items that contributed to an enhanced bottom line.

Reese's support, advice, and encouragement gave us the freedom to really 'fly by the seat of our pants.' As I said before, this was the first business organization to introduce the Principles to their employees. We had no model to follow when we designed the human relations program. We listened to the employees, at all levels, and listened to our wisdom. In a sense, we felt we were blazing a new trail in the business world.

It was such a pleasure working for this company. Chip and I were very grateful for the opportunity to share what we had learned about the Principles, and about how this understanding would enhance the work experience of the employees. After our first session we were so elated, we felt like skipping to the parking lot.

We worked for this firm for approximately five years. Ken partnered with us; he brainstormed with Chip and me as we developed the interview questionnaire, collated the information once it was gathered, and helped prepare the final report. Ken had a unique perspective which was a wonderful addition to our work. Occasionally, during the interview phase, if we had a recalcitrant employee, we would have Ken conduct the interview. His gentle, down to earth manner soon put the individual at ease, which allowed Ken to draw out valuable information.

Toward the end of our time with Reese's business, he offered Ken an in-house position as special projects manager. He sent Ken to an out-of state company division to do some training, but teaching wasn't really Ken's passion. He enjoyed working with his hands, and had a natural talent for organizing things. He ended up helping supervise the construction of a new facility for the company.

Ultimately, when Reese sold the company in 1990, Ken was managing, for the firm, a small woodworking shop that built book and magazine displays. He continued doing this for the new owners of the corporation until he left, toward the end of 1996.

Reese introduced Chip and me to other organizations, for which we provided Principles training. He really paved the way for our work to continue in the Tampa Bay area, and not only in the corporate arena. He was keen on introducing the Three

Principles to disadvantaged communities. To that end, I followed suit.

I had become very interested in the community work Dr. Roger Mills was pioneering in Miami. At a Principles conference, I met the first residents Roger had trained, from the Modello community in Homestead, a short distance from Miami. The residents were impressive; vibrant, confident, passionate about their community, and eager to share stories of how their neighborhood was being transformed by the Principles understanding.

Inspired, I decided to change direction from solely working with business, and try my hand at community work. I had no clue how to do this. When I asked Roger, he simply said, "Listen, and build rapport."

This was the same advice Syd had given Roger when he began to educate the residents on the role of the Principles in creating their experience. Although Roger did have a background in community development, it was based on a traditional model. That framework didn't look at the innate wisdom and resiliency in the residents, but rather focused on what was wrong, and how the consultants could fix it.

Ignoring the old model, Roger introduced the residents to their own inner wisdom, which guided them toward positive solutions for themselves and their community. I loved this aspect and couldn't wait to get started.

After researching and approaching almost every community representative in the Tampa Bay region and finding no interest, I came to the conclusion it wasn't meant to happen, at least not at that time. I saw that my desire to "do" the Principles in communities had created a good deal of stress for me. Letting go of the desire released the stress.

It's amazing what happens when we get out of the way. The very next day, I got a phone call from the president of the Residents' Counsel of an inner city community that had not been on my list. The woman said she heard I had something to do with the Modello project and indicated her interest. Long story short, I ended up conducting a three year program in their community. It was a wonderful experience and set the stage for more community work in Los Angeles, and other cities across America.

After twelve years in Tampa, I was offered a job in Los Angeles, working for the California School of Professional Psychology (CSPP). For several years, prior to this offer, I had been managing various community projects in the United States for Roger Mills and CSPP, through the Health Realization Institute that Roger had initiated at the school. During this time, Volunteers of America became interested in Roger's work, and consequently, I was invited to meet with the CEO and tour the area of Skid Row where their organization had plans to build a homeless drop-in center. After the tour, and after reading the grant, in which they spoke of treating the homeless population as their "guests, with respect and dignity," I knew I was meant to work with this group. *

Ken was all for the move, which surprised me a great deal. He loved Tampa and enjoyed the climate, which offered wonderful boating and both freshwater and ocean fishing, but he was ready for a change. His career as manager of the woodworking shop no longer held his interest; the new corporation which had purchased Reese's company had a totally different corporate philosophy, one that Ken was not comfortable with. So the opportunity for something new appealed to his sense of adventure.

Syd's prediction, that we would travel the world, sharing the message of the Principles, once again was moving us forward—beyond our imagination, to a whole new world. If anyone had told me a year earlier that I'd be moving to California to work with staff and the homeless in Skid Row, for Volunteers of America, I'd have said, "You're dreaming." Yet here we were, with the phrase, "California, here we come" ringing in our ears, moving our belongings across the country to the Golden State.

In March, 2002, after five years in California, our return to Salt Spring Island seemed to complete the circle. We had started off on Salt Spring studying with Syd, and now Ken and I were back. Syd encouraged our move and welcomed us to the island. I was a bit concerned about conducting my business locally, bringing people here for trainings, and so on. I felt Syd might lose some of his privacy; I used Syd's materials for my work so all my clients were familiar with the Principles, and would recognize Syd if they saw him. But Syd assured Ken and me that he would take care of any privacy issues that might occur.

Of course, Syd had been invited to Tampa and Los Angeles by our business group, as well as others, to give seminars and meet with local leaders; so he had continued to be an integral part of our lives. Still, to be living close to him once again added a very special feeling to our lives, and we considered it a privilege.

A new phase began in my work over the next decade. I offered retreats, various training programs, and executive coaching, as well as conducting on-site trainings at corporate locations. I also had the opportunity to travel to other countries. Syd's prediction had definitely come true. I felt I had the best of both worlds—to be living near Syd, to learn from his wisdom, which ignited my own, and to have the honor of sharing what I was learning with the global community.

---

*My previous book, *Our True Identity...Three Principles*, tells more of the story of that first project in Tampa, as well as our move to California, my community work in Los Angeles, and many other examples of the Three Principles' impact.

Part Two

The Principles in Business

More Bang for Your Buck

*I*t is extraordinarily valuable to know that three intrinsic Principles—Mind, Consciousness, and Thought—generate all human experience, and that via these Principles, we have the power to alter our experience of life. This understanding sets us on a life-long path, a journey of adventure; always interesting, sometimes challenging. When I say challenging, I mean in a productive way that moves each of us forward in our development as a human being, and as a leader.

There are well-intentioned leadership programs, even programs that introduce some version of the Principles, which focus on the process and content of thought. They do this based on the premise that by examining what we are thinking, we will be able to change the content of thought, and thus our behavior. However, this emphasis often gets people caught up in cyclical thinking, adding to their stress and busy minds.

There is a far more natural, effective, and simple way to transform human behavior. Recognizing that it is the Principle of Thought that enables people to create experience is the path to true empowerment. The Principle is *before* the form of both individual thoughts and any subsequent behavior.

Occasionally, leadership programs may impart information about consciousness, in terms of being mindful of behavior. This attention to conduct, like focusing on the content of thought, also gets people fixated on the form, and once again, we get off track.

The Principle of Consciousness is the gift of awareness that we are the *creator* of our behavior and our own reality. Being aware we are the *thinker* creating form is very enriching, and far healthier than simply being aware of the form.

Seldom do the types of models mentioned above bring to light the Principle of Mind, the pure formless power behind life and experience. Mind is the spiritual, creative intelligence that is the source of insights, guiding us unerringly into our true nature.

When only one or two Principles are presented, on an intellectual level, we can be left with a gap in our understanding. The gap minimizes our innate, natural power, reducing our mental stability. It's like a bridge without enough timber or concrete underneath to support the structure; in the case of the gap in understanding, the bridge of knowledge needs to be shored up by all Three Principles.

Yes, it's true that getting a glimmer of even one Principle can make an enormous difference in one's life; it happened to me. Nonetheless, it makes sense that having an understanding of the Three Principles adds to the sustainability of our wellbeing.

Here's an example of what I mean. Larry, a young, enthusiastic manager of a Research and Development Division at a manufacturing plant, expressed his respect for the Three Principles this way.

"When a management consulting firm provided the initial training for changing our corporate culture, I got a lot out of the program. For the first time, I considered my thinking a viable tool in modifying my behavior. As I gained some understanding of the role of thought, my interactions with my co-workers began to change. Before the Culture Change Training (CCT), I tended to assume that whatever circumstances occurred, they were the problem. I didn't realize that it was my *thinking* about the circumstances that really made the difference. CCT went a long way in helping me cope with stress on the job, and at home.

"But there came a point when I felt I had gotten all I could out of the CCT program, and wondered if I was missing something. The fact is, I wasn't maintaining my mental clarity or healthy state of mind. My moods fluctuated and I felt at a loss. I had been so pumped on what I had learned with CCT that it was disappointing to realize this knowledge didn't seem to last.

"Then I was introduced to the Three Principles training and was educated on the fact there are Three Principles that generate our experience. Somehow that seemed to resonate within me.

"I learned about Consciousness and how this Principle helps us always be aware that we are the *thinker*, and therefore in charge of our life. When we give our attention to negative thoughts, a negative reality is what we produce. If we focus our attention in a positive manner, a healthy reality is produced. Even when we experience challenges or traumatic times, if we can think about these situations from a balanced perspective, we are more likely to come up with a common sense solution.

"I learned about the principle of Mind, the source of power behind life, a formless energy that we, as human beings, have the ability to turn into form, into the form of behavior, and of our personal reality. This was very exciting to me. As an engineer, I am fascinated by the notion of pure energy and I wanted to learn more about how to turn the formless energy into form.

"That's when it clicked for me that the Principle of Thought is the vehicle for turning formless energy into the form of behavior. With our thoughts, we have the power to create our experience and our behavior. I began to see that when I was operating from a healthy state of mind, automatically my life was smoother. I didn't have to *examine* my thinking and *try* to think positive. I was already doing that, automatically and naturally. It blew my mind!

"I discovered that my mental health was more constant. Do I still have times of stress and frustration? You bet I do. But the stressful periods are not as intense and don't last as long. The awareness that I am the thinker helps defuse the intensity of stressful emotions. I have become more the observer of my thinking instead of the victim of my thoughts. With this knowledge, I've begun to make better choices. I realize the difference between being aware of behavior and being aware that I *create* the behavior.

"The knowledge that there are Three Principles at work inside of us, and that we can count on them, has been a life saver. I never knew we had such a powerful internal system that we operate. I used to feel the best I could do was cope with life, and I did pretty well with coping. Now, I feel like I'm thriving on life. I feel like I've got more 'bang for my buck' and am no longer shortchanged by only having part of the picture."

From Source of Irritation to Superstar

$\mathcal{T}$he dynamics of how people change are fascinating. Sometimes the change happens in the subtlest way. The catalyst can be a mentally healthy person conversing, from a non-judgmental position, with someone who is living in a world of stress. The innate health and compassion emanating from one individual has the power to touch the inner core of another.

Let me give you an example from my business coaching experience:

Carolyn, a chemical engineer, was very bright and very competent in her field; however, her interactions with colleagues left something to be desired. She was critical of her co-workers, demanding of her support staff, and brooked no nonsense from anyone, including her boss. Many in her department felt Carolyn was a source of irritation.

At the same time, Carolyn was sensitive to the nuances of tension coming from her co-workers, and took this as a sign of disrespect toward her. She felt her co-workers were rude, inattentive and uncooperative. Carolyn did not understand what she contributed to the situation. She didn't hear herself speaking in a disrespectful tone of voice to those around her, or being accusatory when things weren't done according to her standards.

Carolyn was like a fish in a fish bowl, seeing only her world through her eyes; she was not open to others' perspectives or opinions. The irony of the situation was that Carolyn's unhealthy conduct unconsciously stressed her, as well as irritating others.

One of Carolyn's co-workers, Tony, had gone through Three Principles training and was in a very healthy state of mind. Being mentally healthy, Tony's presence and conversation offered Carolyn some respite, giving her a mental break from her exasperating habits, and the reactions they usually produced. Tony did not take Carolyn's manner personally and saw beyond her behavior to the heart of his colleague; he saw that she, like everyone, had the potential for mental well-being.

Consequently, Tony was able to maintain a healthy relationship with Carolyn. Because he saw her psychological innocence; that she was unaware of her annoying habit of treating people with apparent disdain, Tony felt compassion for her. In his compassion, he had no judgment, and the neutrality of feeling provided a working environment that allowed Carolyn to naturally feel better, even without understanding why her stress was decreasing.

Their conversations occasionally touched on the principle of Thought and how our thoughts create our behaviors and emotions. Tony expressed his appreciation for the principle of Mind, which provides guidance for us in our lives. Tony explained how *noticing* the negative pull of unhealthy stress lessens the intensity of the stress, and he tied this ability to the principle of Consciousness.

These nuggets of information intrigued Carolyn and she became increasingly curious about how Tony maintained his healthy perspective, despite organizational changes that affected everyone's positions. She told Tony that she considered him "unflappable" and wondered how he managed to stay calm during the harried pace that was often a part of their work situation. She told him she wished she were more like him.

As time passed, Carolyn had some insights that changed her thinking; she became more positive, which improved interactions with her co-workers and colleagues. She was able to contribute more productively to her job; she came up with creative solutions to long-standing issues, and was more open to input from others. Carolyn was in service to her team in a way she never had been before.

She shared her new thoughts with Tony, "When you change the way you look at things, the things you look at seem to change. I never realized this before and always looked to other people to change. I felt my way was the right way. Now I'm finding that as I listen to my team more, we get more done together. There isn't the tension of competition there used to be. Everyone is pulling for the optimal solution, and happy to share the credit."

Her co-workers noticed that Carolyn was much easier to get along with, and enthusiastically included her in team meetings, without reservation. They saw her becoming the team leader and applauded her innovative ideas. She drew the team together, and they brainstormed collectively, each building on the others' thoughts, working cooperatively to achieve their goals. Carolyn was on her way to becoming a "superstar" in the department, and the same was said of the team.

Sound far-fetched? You may think so, but through the years, I have seen many such stories. Just consider the possibility; change can occur with simplicity and subtlety. It doesn't take much to elicit wisdom and common sense from people, primarily because these resources are already within us all.

Wisdom does not come from the brain or from memory. It is released naturally by slowing down our thinking; by having a quiet mind. In Carolyn's case, Tony's calm presence and acceptance helped her mind to become quieter, and his occasional references to the Principles were like seeds planted in fertile soil.

One "Aha" moment—such as Carolyn's realization about her interactions with others—is evidence that wisdom comes via insight, not from memory. An insight is an original thought we have never had before, and it can slip through our usual thinking via even an instant of mental stillness.

Slow down—and wisdom will emerge, allowing any one of us to become a "superstar"!

A New Perspective on Rapport

"*I*s it possible to have rapport with someone you may not like?"

"Is it possible to have rapport with someone you may not trust?"

These questions came out in a group discussion regarding the merits of rapport, in the context of organizational leadership. I was invited to sit in, merely as an observer, and would like to share some of the conversation I observed with you.

Colin: "It seems to me that if you don't like someone, it would be impossible to have rapport with that person. As far as not trusting someone and still having rapport, I can't see that either. That is an unreasonable notion."

Many heads nodded in agreement and voiced the same opinion.

Diane: "I'm just thinking...in the context of the Three Principles, the definition of rapport is seeing beyond behavior, to the person's innate mental health. If we were *seeing* with that kind of understanding, wouldn't that give us the ability to have rapport with anyone? I don't know; I'm just asking."

Stuart: "I think of rapport as being on the same wavelength with someone, which comes with a harmonious feeling. How can you have that with someone you don't like or respect?"

Colin: "Yeah!"

Diane: "As we're talking, it occurs to me there have been a few occasions when I've felt a sort of neutral connection for someone I didn't think I liked or trusted. The neutral feeling was more a feeling of understanding, where I saw beyond their behavior to their core, to the humanity of the individual. As I recall, when I felt that neutrality, there wasn't a question of like or dislike, trust or mistrust; it was just an impersonal feeling. I wasn't engaged in judging their behavior, or attached to outcome. And I discovered that most times, I liked the person."

Stuart: "When you say 'impersonal,' it sounds cold and standoffish. That's not how I think of rapport."

Diane: "Let me put it this way; when I first learned to drive a standard transmission, I ground a lot of gears. This was hard on the gears and the engine. Once I learned to shift smoothly, the gears didn't get as much wear and tear; so naturally, they lasted longer and performed better.

"This is how I see having a more neutral state of mind; being able to shift from judgment, without grinding on things that stress me out. Neutrality helps me be more understanding of people, and not take things so personally. In this neutral, healthy state of mind, I'm not so demanding of others; I see their potential. When I speak to their potential rather than to their behavior, their work performance improves."

Colin: "Nonsense!"

Diane: "Ah, come on, Colin. I heard you the other day talking to your grandson on the phone. You told me later he'd had an accident with your truck; that he'd been drinking and ran into the ditch. You said no one was hurt but the vehicle was badly damaged. You were so good with him on the phone. You didn't lose your temper; you let him know he was responsible for fixing the damage and that you'd be talking with him later. I thought the way you handled him was wonderful."

Colin: "Yeah, but he's my grandson and I like him. I may not trust him with the truck for a while. . .

Stuart: "I think I can see where Diane is heading. You saw beyond your grandkid's behavior, and you talked to the grown up part of him, in terms of his responsibility for fixing the truck. But you didn't lose your temper. In other words, you kept rapport with him."

Colin: "I tell you that is a completely different situation. He's my grandson."

Diane: "But suppose you could have that feeling of objectivity with more of your employees? Wouldn't that be helpful?"

Colin: "I'm out of here. I've gotta go back to work."

Stuart to Diane after Colin had left the room: "Well, Colin certainly took our conversation to heart, didn't he?"

Diane: "I think he was ticked off; I don't know about his taking anything we said to heart."

Stuart: "The way you kept your rapport with Colin impressed me, Diane. You walked your talk. And Colin is a good guy. I've known him a long time and I know he'll be thinking over what was said today. Give him some time. Maybe he'll surprise you. As for me, I've found our conversation thought provoking, and look forward to our next meeting."

As an observer, I was fascinated by this discussion. What particularly impressed me was that the feeling of respect, and the depth of Diane and Stuart's listening, remained constant throughout the meeting. Clearly, at the beginning, there was a significant difference in how each person thought. Yet as Diane kept her bearings, Stuart began to *see* what she was saying. She didn't try to convince anyone; she simply remained open and yet strong in her wisdom.

At the end, it was interesting to me that when Colin abruptly left the room and Diane wondered if he'd heard anything, Stuart was the one who counseled Diane. Rapport, *seeing* beyond behavior, definitely was working its magic with this group.

The Sandpaper Effect of Consciousness

*T*he Principle of Consciousness continues to amaze me with its infinite power, as it unfolds a multi-faceted awareness of how humans create experience. It is an extraordinary spiritual gift. Once a glimmer of Consciousness reveals our true nature, this gift is always readily available to help us.

Sometimes we forget that our personal consciousness is part of the Principle of Consciousness, and as such, has a wealth of guidance to draw upon, whether we choose to do so or not.

If we pay attention to the gentle nudging of our inner common sense, consciousness can have a productive impact on our quality of life. If we choose not to pay attention, the gentle nudging may become a bit more insistent.

When we are in a low mood, we often choose not to listen to our wisdom. This is when the proddings of our enhanced consciousness can feel like sandpaper, rubbing us the wrong way.

Just as a carpenter uses sandpaper on wood, to smooth away roughness and reveal the fine grain beneath the surface; so does our consciousness dispel the layers of ego and negative thoughts, exposing a finer, clearer state of mind. The clarity provides a new outlook on life. As deeper understanding occurs, we begin to feel better. Our consciousness is elevated, and guides us in resolving the issues that may have seemed insurmountable from a lower level.

For example, Charlotte, a leadership development trainer who is learning about the Principles, had been having a difficult time integrating her new understanding of the Principles into the framework of her traditional training modules. The techniques she was familiar with weren't having the same impact in her classes.

Charlotte told me, during a coaching session, that even when she was nervous talking to her team about what she had learned and experienced in regard to the Principles, her audience was alert and attentive. She did admit, with a wry tone, that there were some who wondered what planet she was from, given the information she was imparting; but for the most part, her enthusiasm about what she is learning fired up the group. Some of them wanted to learn more about the ground-breaking paradigm she was sharing.

In addition to her new zest and vitality, Charlotte was having better results with her clients, which evoked more curiosity from her colleagues. When she tried to tell them what she had learned, she tended to get flustered and tongue-tied, finding it difficult to explain to them the power of the Principles.

As Charlotte related this to me, she was articulate in describing what was most meaningful to her about the Principles. "I see Mind, Consciousness and Thought as the foundation of my work, and my life. These Principles feel right to me, as if I've always known about them inside, but didn't know how to express them.

"I'm beginning to see more clearly that I create my experience. This has empowered me not to take things so personally; although I will say I find it challenging not to get gripped by the disbelief some of my coworkers express. People in my firm are very systematic; I've often felt out of step in this company, and judged myself harshly. I've created a lot of angst for myself trying to fit into the analytical mold. After all, this is how I was trained."

"What is your wisdom telling you about this situation?" I asked.

"I'm feeling like I'm on a see-saw. One day I feel on top of the world, that I've discovered something as precious as the Three Principles, and I appreciate everyone I come into contact with. When my mind is clear, I can see I've been trying too hard with my colleagues. I need to just relax, be myself, and let the results of my work speak for themselves."

There was a long pause, as she gathered her thoughts. "I see that I'm trying to mix the Principles with the traditional models of leadership development; I know that isn't the way to go. I know these Principles stand alone; they are fundamental to human functioning—they are not techniques.

"Yet, in the next moment," Charlotte continued, "I am berating myself for not taking life more seriously, and telling myself that I need to come to grips with reality, and fit within the traditional system. But it just doesn't feel right," she said in a discouraged tone.

"I can't seem to get away from an inner feeling that life is not a technique; to continue to use the technique oriented models is doing a disservice to my clients. To me, the Principles are a gift, and an inherent benefit of life. I'm just not sure how to go about sharing what I've learned," she ended dolefully.

My heart was touched by Charlotte's story. I felt she was doing an amazing job, considering the situation she was in, trying to adjust her new perspective within a traditional organization.

"I think you're doing far more than you realize, Charlotte. You have so much integrity—holding strong to what you know is right. And your own wisdom is telling you to just be yourself in regard to sharing what you're learning with your co-workers."

I held Charlotte's gaze as I said, "When you don't listen, it doesn't feel good, because you know better—it seems to me that you are experiencing the sandpaper effect of your own consciousness on your belief system. That's a good thing; the sandpaper is sanding down your old belief system, exposing more wisdom, which is supporting and sustaining your new understanding.

"When you talk to me about what you're learning, Charlotte, you're clear and expressive in your description. Your words ring true. So I support your instinct in trusting yourself to be who you are now; that feeling of security and confidence will attract your colleagues more than anything you could say.

"You're right, Charlotte, when you say you can't integrate the Principles with traditional models or techniques. That's why it doesn't feel right to you. Techniques are form and static while the Principles are before form. Your heightened consciousness is alerting you to this fact.

"When you trust your wisdom," I continued, "you will find that you can talk in the moment, beyond thought, and you will be relevant to your audience. The deep feeling you experience will help draw out the innate wisdom from those you are speaking to, allowing insights to emerge. This is a new way of learning, without a developed structure or module, but more a framework being created in the moment, and then released when you're finished with it."

I hesitated, as I assessed how much more she could take, and then continued. "Let me ask you this, Charlotte. What is the result of your feeling on top of the world and appreciative of everyone?"

Charlotte paused for a long moment as she reflected on my question. "I'm having some wonderful conversations with people, and my relationships are improving as I take things less personally. My enhanced relationships are the basis for deeper rapport, honesty and trust with my clients.

"I see that my clients are also developing their leadership qualities, based more on relationships than on technical skills. Don't get me wrong, their technical skills are improving as well, but it is their ability to listen more deeply to their teams, with less judgment, that is really creating change in their departments.

Their employees are not intimidated or insecure about coming to the managers to discuss whatever needs to be discussed—success or failure. They don't feel the need to cover their mistakes anymore. They have the confidence to admit when they've made an error and take responsibility for it."

There was a silence while we both absorbed Charlotte's comments. Suddenly, Charlotte burst out laughing. "I just realized the sandpaper effect is smoothing my clients' rough spots into healthier states of mind, too. They are learning about the Principles, just as I am, and becoming more aware. Their new found consciousness is leading to improved behavior, naturally, without addressing the behavior. This is so exciting!" she said, her eyes sparkling with delight.

"I had no idea things were going so well until I started to talk with you. Now it's all coming to light. Our lives are enhanced from sanding down our rough spots. Sandpaper effect, indeed," Charlotte concluded with a smile.

Beyond Techniques

One of the most beautiful places on Salt Spring is the Tsawout First Nations Reserve Land, down the road across from Beaver Point Hall. While this land is still used by the Tsawout people on various occasions, they generously grant the gift of public access to its trails and beaches most of the time.

The property overlooks the ocean passageway that gradually turns into Fulford Harbour, where the ferry to and from Victoria docks. Ken and I often hike the trails in the reserve because the scenery is so spectacular and the ambience of the place evokes peace and tranquility.

One place of particular interest, midway along the trail, is a small clearing surrounded by towering firs, cedars and the occasional rare Garry oak tree. As you enter the area, you're compelled to stop, not knowing why. A sense of stillness pervades. As you slowly move forward, you see in the center of the clearing a short tree stump, its base circled by old fallen branches, overlapping one other. The top of the stump is covered with natural treasures: tiny seashells, unusual colored stones, fragments of driftwood, and shredded tobacco left as gifts, simply in honor of the privilege of walking through the land. It feels like a sacred place.

Further along the trail you come to a cove with a pebble beach, protected by a rocky point immersed in the ocean. If the tide is out, you may see huge starfish there, clinging to the rock outcropping; purple, red, orange, brilliant colors displayed against the granite colored stone.

This Native Land Reserve is a place I've taken clients when they've come to the island to learn more about the Principles. I know that people absorb more when they are relaxed and their minds are quiet. Such an occasion occurred for two women, business executives who had come to meet with me for personal and professional development. We had spent some productive time together on the first day, and on the second day, rather than meeting once again in the conference room I'd arranged for our sessions, I suggested we explore a bit of the island. They enthusiastically agreed, and after changing into casual clothes, off we went.

Following a twenty minute drive, we arrived and started our walk to the pebble beach. The women loved the natural setting. As we came to the small clearing with the remnant of the tree, they too were halted at the entrance, as if by an invisible band of energy, before they slowly stepped in. It was like a door opening into this mystical silence. We stood motionless for a time, absorbing this special place; not a word was spoken. Finally, with a glance at each other in acknowledgment of the quietude, we carried on down the trail toward the beach.

The women, Lucy and Fran, were absolutely delighted to see the tide out and the starfish exhibiting their beauty on the rock promontory. After numerous photos were taken, we sat on the beach, backs resting against an old log.

"This is paradise," Lucy stated. "I'm so glad that our company was agreeable to us coming here to work with you. I feel I learned a good deal yesterday, but today I seem to be absorbing more and we've not even talked about anything to do with work. I just feel great."

Fran was nodding her head in agreement, her face beaming with good humor and health. "In the past, I felt I had to practice techniques in order to change, to develop myself, personally and professionally. I found that if I did not continue to engage in the use of techniques, I would quickly revert to my old patterns of life and forget the ideas I had learned.

"For example, I used to love the affirmation technique, where you tell yourself over and over again, 'I am a great leader;' or 'I can do this difficult task;' or 'I will be successful in my career.'

"But frankly, I began to be bored by the routine of talking to myself," Fran chuckled. "And after a while I didn't believe it, because nothing was really changing, at least not permanently. If I forgot to affirm how great I was, I would feel depressed. Something inside told me this process wasn't helpful.

"Then I learned about the Three Principles. I discovered that the Principles are a natural part of who we are. I realized that I honestly didn't need to 'condition' myself to be happy or successful. Those attributes are already within me."

Lucy had been listening quietly to her friend. I could see she was very moved by her friend's words. We sat quietly for a few minutes watching as the ferry approached Fulford Harbour; then Lucy spoke.

"It seems to me that we ARE the Principles in action. If we trust that, relax, and just live, it appears to me that our lives will unfold as they are meant to.

"I know, since I've been learning about the Principles, my life and work have improved in ways I could never have imagined. I'm so grateful to have had just a glimmer of our true nature. Somehow that glimmer has transformed my life.

"I used to think I needed to intellectually understand how one changes one's habits of thought and belief systems. Now I am seeing that relaxing into your true self is how the Principles become more visible. Then the understanding comes from an insight, from inner wisdom. This mystical process is so much gentler and easier than studying techniques, trying so hard to improve yourself. Frankly, I found trying to better myself hard work and exhausting. I was always judging myself and others. When you're always trying, there's no room for 'being,'" Lucy declared emphatically.

Rising suddenly, Lucy reached out a hand to her friend, pulling her to her feet. "Let's walk back and go for lunch now. I'm starving!"

My heart was full as I watched these two women walk ahead of me, up the pathway to the top of the hill where our car was parked. They were so spirited in their love of learning and, clearly, they had learned a lot that would continue to guide them on their journey in life. My job had been to point them to their true nature which they had joyfully embraced. Now they were well equipped to handle whatever came their way.

Our Inner Guidance

*W*e have so much to be grateful for in our lifetime. Many technological advances benefit the world today; but more importantly, we are privileged to be sharing with humanity a new paradigm in mental health. Knowing we have the power to create our moment-to-moment experience, via the Three Principles, is an essential discovery, a divine gift, and our birthright.

It is significant to note that the Principles—Mind, Consciousness and Thought—are neutral in themselves. With our free will, and using the Three Principles, we can make our personal reality whatever we want. Until we understand how to use the Principles wisely, there are pros and cons to having free will; but that's the name of the game—learning how to use this gift with respect and with love. When our frame of mind is stable, our life corresponds—when our mood is low, our life can become filled with drama.

We have freedom of mind to choose how to respond to any situation. It is powerful, as well as comforting, to know we can rely on our natural, inner wisdom to guide us, no matter what circumstances come our way. Our intrinsic common sense is always available; the only thing that keeps us from listening to it is our faulty thinking, holding us prisoner to misguided ideas. Realizing we don't have to be a victim of our stressful thoughts is invaluable. Once we gain clarity, via insight, we are as free as the air we breathe.

Let me give you an example to consider. This story was related by Kevin, a colleague of mine.

Andy had been having a tough time at work. His level of frustration was very high, and at one point, he erupted. He cursed out his boss, stomped out of work and headed for home. Andy's boss called Kevin, the company's employee assistance counselor. The boss asked Kevin to talk with Andy to help him calm down, and to educate him on the benefits of the Principles and innate mental health. Happy to do so, Kevin arranged a meeting.

"Tell me a little about yourself, Andy."

"Well, I guess you could say I'm having a nervous break-down. I find myself out of control. Just the other day, I cussed out my boss and stormed out of work. My mind was racing so furiously driving home, I was lucky to make it there in one piece. I banged the car door getting out, slammed the front door as I went inside, said 'Hi' to my wife, and stomped upstairs to bed."

"I see. Is there anything more you wish to tell me?"

"The next day I felt a bit better and knew I had to apologize to my boss. He took it well; didn't get bent out of shape with me. I give him a lot of credit that he didn't fire me on the spot."

"That's a lot of wisdom you've shown," Kevin commented.

"What? How do you figure that? I just told you how I blew it and you're saying that's wise! I don't get you," Andy said emphatically.

"Let's look at the situation from another angle, Andy. Look at what you did right once you got home."

Andy paused for a moment, frowned, and then said, "I don't see anything right about what I did when I got home."

"You told me you said 'Hi' to your wife and then went directly to bed, right?"

"That's right."

"You didn't take your anger and frustration out on your wife, is that correct?"

"Well, yes," Andy said reluctantly.

"Then you went to bed; have I got that right?"

Again, Andy said hesitantly, "Yes. I was just so beat that I collapsed on the bed. I don't see what's so wise about that."

"You also apologized to your boss."

"Well, yeah. I still want my job."

"How did you know to do all those things—not yell at your wife, go to bed and rest, apologize to your boss—in the midst of this so-called nervous breakdown? That's some breakdown, I must say; to still have so much common sense in the midst of that episode. You did a lot of damage control."

Andy remained silent, looking perplexed.

Kevin paused, considered his client, and then continued, "Everyone has innate mental health, or common sense, built into them. We're born with this capacity. We also have three inherent Principles with which we create our experience. We wouldn't exist without these three gifts. The trick is to learn how to use them appropriately for our benefit, rather than against ourselves."

"I've never heard of the Three Principles you mention; and I'm not sure that I create my experience. This is news to me. My work has been really stressful lately. There are a lot of new projects coming in, requiring complex technology, and I'm feeling overwhelmed by it all. The way I've always seen it, events happen and we react to them; that's what I'm doing. I've tried to cope with things but I've just gotten more stressed. I never thought of my situation in the terms you describe," Andy replied thoughtfully.

Kevin continued to teach Andy about the Principles and how we use them to construct our moment to moment experience. He emphasized that Andy had already had a taste of his own wisdom; he just hadn't realized it at the time. Kevin pointed out the benefits of learning how the Principles work, so Andy would have a better handle on where his psychological experience came from, giving him more control over his emotional state.

Kevin paused to allow some quiet time for Andy to absorb all that had been said. A peace filled the room as the men connected at a deeper level.

After a while, Kevin gently interrupted the silence, saying, "I'd like you to envision a new way of looking at yourself, Andy. I'd like you to consider that you have more wisdom than you give yourself credit for."

Shaking his head as if bemused, Andy said, "It never occurred to me there was anything good to be seen in this event. I'm puzzled; how did I know how to do damage control? I thought I was completely 'out to lunch.' However, as you point out the things I did right, I have to agree. Yet I didn't think about doing those things. It just seemed to happen naturally."

"That exactly right! That's what I'm talking about," Kevin exclaimed animatedly. "Now you're getting it. As you said, 'It just seemed to happen naturally'."

"I feel this is a good place to end our session for today, Andy. You've heard a lot. Let's talk again next week. In the meantime, I'd like you to reflect on the fact that despite your so-called nervous breakdown, your innate health was still functioning, and kept you from doing too much damage. Are you willing to do this?"

"It's something for me to mull over. I can't quite get my head around these Principles you're talking about, but I'd like to learn more. I've never thought I had what you're calling 'innate wisdom' inside of me. I know I've got good sense about some of the familiar technological requirements of my work, but this inner stuff you're telling me about is something new; I'm going to have to sit with it. Although, I must say, since talking with you I do feel calmer, and more hopeful that I'm doing something right," Andy said with a sigh of relief.

"I'll tell you something, Andy, I don't completely understand these Principles myself, not by a long shot; but I see the results, over and over again, in my life and in my clients' lives, and that's what tells me they're real.

"Look for positive feelings; they'll guide you to your wisdom. If your feelings are negative, don't try and figure it out. That's a trap. Simply slow down and let your wisdom rise to the surface once again. That's the secret, Andy; that's where the answers are."

Andy's workplace is lucky; they have in place an employee assistance program, based on the Three Principles. It's part of their corporate culture. They call it "healthy high performance."

Knowing that our feelings reflect our state of mind provides a clue to maintaining well-being. Our inner guide is always available to bring us back to wisdom. Isn't that reassuring? No matter how lost we might find ourselves, we always have the capacity to find our way back to mental health.

An example of this is the fact that Andy, naturally guided by his wisdom, intuitively knew not to dig himself into a deeper hole by picking a fight with his wife when he got home, and so on.

A reader may ask, "What about others who would pick a fight with the wife, and wouldn't apologize to the boss?"

To this, I would say: each person's response to a situation reflects their level of consciousness and their free will. The more we learn, the more we come to realize we have a choice in how we conduct ourselves. This is what's so exciting about sharing the innovative paradigm of the Three Principles; letting more of the world know everyone has a choice, everyone has an inner guide.

Imagine if more organizations, communities, and families learned about the innate gift of wisdom, residing within each and every one. The world would soon be a different place.

Being in Integrity

The title of this article came from an interesting phone conversation I had with a client, Paul. Our dialogue elicited insights
for both of us. We were discussing the spiritual nature of the
Three Principles, and how important it is to reflect on what the
Principles *are* as well as what the Principles *do*. Paul is a department manager at a manufacturing plant. He is keen to introduce
the Principles to his team but uncertain how to explain them.

"I find it difficult to articulate the Three Principles to my
team," Paul related. "The results I've experienced in my life are
transformative; but when I try to tell others, I end up making a
mess of it. Some of my team have commented on the difference
in my leadership style. They tell me I listen more and am less
reactive. My lead supervisor asked if I'd had some special education that they hadn't heard about. They kid me about my level
of calmness, saying that a bomb could go off and I'd calmly tell
them to vacate the premises. I know there is interest in how I've
achieved this level of composure and the ability to manage my
employees better. Yet when they ask me how I've accomplished
and sustained what they call my "unflappable" state of mind, I
find myself getting very wordy and complex in my explanation.
Their eyes cross and soon they find something else to do. I'm just
about at my wits end! I want to be in integrity to what I know
and what I feel, but I'm not quite sure how to go about it. Do
you have any advice?"

"I appreciate your situation, Paul. It's a common question, brought up by a lot of people in the same boat as you. Let me ask you this: What has been most meaningful to you about the Three Principles?"

"Hmm. Good question. I'd have to say the first thing that struck me was the realization that my thoughts create my reality. I, as so many others, believed that circumstances created my reality, and I had to deal with the situation as best I could. Usually there was only one way to deal with life. It was my way or the highway," Paul said ruefully. "Needless to say, this rough approach caused me a good deal of difficulty with my family, and to be honest, created push back at the plant with my colleagues and the workforce.

"Once I had my eyes opened to the fact that I create my experience by the way I view life, my perspective shifted and so did my experience. My understanding of how people function also took a giant leap, and I stopped taking things so personally. I could see that people were doing their best, given their thinking in the moment, so I responded rather than reacting."

"Why don't you share with your team what you just shared with me? You were brief and articulate in your description. I didn't find you wordy or complex."

There was a long pause as Paul pondered my comment. "It's when I come to describe what the Principles are that I get into trouble. I have such a deep feeling that the Principles are spiritual in nature, that they operate before the form of behavior and experience. But there is no way I can explain that to my team— nor do I care to delve into the spiritual aspect of life with them at work. It doesn't seem appropriate. It feels like I would be pushing religion or something like that. I don't consider myself religious, but there are many at work who are and I wouldn't want to step on their toes."

I could see that Paul was struggling with the dilemma of being true to what he felt, and at the same time having respect for the beliefs of other people; particularly in a work environment where there may be many different religions. I considered him to be an honest and sensitive man.

"I understand that, Paul, and I applaud your common sense. I really can't tell you what to say to your group; it's not my place to do so. I know that your wisdom will guide you in the most appropriate manner that is specifically relevant to you and your team.

"However, I will offer you a suggestion. There is a way you can convey that there is something deeper to life than the form of behavior. To do so, you must listen deeply, and observe where you can make a connection."

"What do you mean, Elsie? You've lost me," Paul stated.

"I mean, connect the spiritual nature of the Principles to something in your team's experience, to provide relevance.

"For example: when I was given a tour of your manufacturing plant, I observed a huge hydraulic press at work. A magnetic arm picked up a flat piece of metal and placed it on a form of a door. When the magnetic arm pulled back, the hydraulic press came down and shaped a door from the flat piece of metal. The hydraulic energy created a form out of the metal. You can't see the hydraulic energy, but you see the results of it."

I paused, waiting for Paul's response. Silence lingered.

"In the same way," I went on, "you can't see the Universal energy of Thought, but you see the results shaped via our thoughts."

There was a deep stillness as Paul considered my example. "What you say is very interesting. I never thought of it like that. It's clear to me. I can see a link between the hydraulic energy and the form of the door that was shaped by the hydraulic force."

There was another long pause before he continued, "But as soon as I started to try and figure it out, the understanding vanished. Isn't that curious," Paul noted.

"Your intellect is slower than an insight," I offered. "Just absorb your insight and don't over think it. Let it marinate and—"

Paul broke in excitedly. "You know what just occurred to me? An idea is pure energy. You don't see the idea until you take action and bring the idea to life."

"That's right. An idea is a thought and we have the power to make a thought real. You can't see the thought, but you see the results of the thought."

"This is fascinating. Something else came to mind. As an engineer, I was taught the engineering principle of Force equals Mass times Acceleration. The equation is: $F = M\,A$. You can't see the Force, which is pure energy, but if you were hit by a truck you'd sure feel it!"

We both burst out laughing at the absurdity, and at the same time, the profundity of our conversation. A natural hush ensued and we could hear each other breathing on the phone. Then Paul ended the quiet reflection. "I need time to absorb this conversation. I've never gone so deep into the spiritual nature of the Principles and connected them to so many other things, like engineering principles. Could we carry on this conversation in a week or so?"

"Absolutely," I agreed. "I also need time to soak up our discussion." We scheduled a time and concluded our call.

The next day I met with Sydney Banks, the originator of the Three Principles, and shared some of the conversation with him; no names or specific details, just the general talk on different aspects of formless energy.

I was still quite excited about the exchange with my client and blathered on to Syd about hydraulic energy. He listened without interruption, with an enigmatic look on his face. When I finally stopped for breath, he looked keenly at me and said, *"The energy you are talking about is not formless. Hydraulic energy still has form but it comes from Universal energy that has no form. Everything comes from Universal energy."*

"Oh", I responded, feeling chastened without knowing why. "I don't understand."

"*Yes, I know*", responded Syd kindly. "*Don't worry about it. It sounds like a fascinating conversation. Just know there is more, much more to learn.*"

After the chat with Syd, my mind ruminated over what he'd said about hydraulic energy coming from Universal energy, before the form of all things. My brain struggled to comprehend his statement until I finally gave up, realizing I was mentally tired—a signal that I was trying to figure it out, just like Paul had, rather than trusting insight.

I decided to go for a walk to clear my head and as I was walking, all of a sudden I felt an excitement course through my veins. It didn't matter that I didn't understand what Syd talked about. It was the feeling I got just considering the depth of what he was saying. The power of his words opened my mind and that was sufficient. An open mind is a mind ready for insight. I almost floated home, happy to be learning something new. I was not able to define what that something new was and I didn't care. I trusted that the learning would reveal itself to me in good time.

Paul and I carried on our discussion a week later, as agreed. I related as well as I could my new learning, inspired by Syd, regarding the fact that all energy—hydraulic, magnetic, electric, and so on—comes from Universal energy, which is before the form of the other energies. I was clear with him that I didn't really understand this, and knew there was more to it than I could articulate. I suggested he read Syd's book, "The Enlightened Gardener Revisited," which talks a great deal about Universal energy.

Paul mentioned he had already read it since our last conversation, and found it very exciting. He noted that the book was one he would treasure and read again and again. "I have something to share with you," Paul went on. "I've been able to talk with my group much more easily. I don't even think about what I'm going to say anymore. It just comes naturally.

"I don't dwell on the spiritual nature of the Principles, but somehow I make my point in ways that captivate my team. It amazes me that when you take the time to listen and to talk deeply with people, most have a sense there is more to life than the physical manifestation. They just don't talk much about it.

"This morning our group conversation went to a very deep level. It was an amazing discussion; we were talking about how something so intangible as the Principles can be so practical; and how this understanding is changing individuals' attitudes, leading to improved team interactions. We all agreed that we're 'jelling' more cohesively and on the road to further success. Consequently, we've decided to meet regularly once a month, just to explore the Three Principles and the insights we're gaining.

"I would never have believed you could have this kind of conversation at work; there was a lot of laughter, as well as some powerful insights. Some other staff members stopped me in the hall after the meeting, and asked me what on earth was going on. They wondered if someone had won the lottery!" Spontaneous laughter erupted from Paul, and I joined him in delight.

Hopefully, more people will acknowledge that there is more to life than what we see; much more. To acknowledge our true source can only bring more knowledge, and who can say 'No' to that?

Thriving versus Surviving

*W*e live in a world where many are fraught with anxiety. The economy is still struggling to make positive gains, unemployment is high, the wars continue, health care issues here and abroad continue to draw a great deal of rancor; it is indeed an uncertain world we live in. Is there a way to thrive in this global environment? Is there a way to thrive in a chaotic organizational situation? Can people thrive versus survive? I'll leave you to come up with your own answers, after you read this chapter.

A fascinating conversation with a client elicited some inner reflection for both of us. Derek called to get help with several issues he was facing in his workplace. He'd had some Three Principles training, and knew I wouldn't talk to him about the issues per se; he knew our dialogue would revolve around the Principles and the gift of innate wisdom. In our earlier conversations, he'd often experienced his mind quieting down, allowing insights and solutions to emerge from his inner common sense. Derek told me he simply wanted me to be a neutral sounding board; to listen. I was happy to comply.

"Our work environment is pretty crazy right now," Derek began. "The stress is very high. The company is laying off employees at all levels, as our industry struggles to survive.

"The executive team I'm on seems to be reverting back to previously held beliefs, and are entrenched in keeping home office happy, without having a say in far reaching decision making. I know they are concerned about their jobs as well.

"We discuss in our meetings how to better serve our employees, but there doesn't seem to be an answer; at least not an answer the team will listen to. I've tried talking with them about how this is the time to listen to our people, not shut them down. I know if we listen to them, at least they'll feel heard, even if we can't necessarily do what they ask.

"As department head, I find myself in the middle. I get heat from my boss when my team doesn't produce, and I get heat from my team and the employees when they feel the decisions coming from corporate don't make sense. There is a great deal of drama going on. How do we get along in this kind of culture?"

"What helps you stay out of the drama?" I asked Derek.

"I don't know," Derek replied. "I guess I stick to the facts of the situation as best as I can. I listen; I don't lay blame, judge or make assumptions. I try and help my team not to 'make up stories' that perpetuate the condition."

"That's a lot of common sense you've just shared with me, Derek. That must help your team and the employees a great deal."

He was slow to respond. "Do you see that, Derek? That you're helping those around you, probably more than you realize?"

"Well I've not really thought about it," he hesitantly answered. "I'm in the midst of this chaotic mental and physical environment all the time, so I don't get a chance to reflect much."

"I'd like to share something with you, Derek. I had a coaching call yesterday with a supervisor in your facility. She told me that one day when you met her in the cafeteria, she was very agitated. You stopped and asked her how she was doing, and she promptly bent your ear with all that was wrong in the department. She said you just listened and didn't advise her until you parted, leaving her with these words, 'Just use your common sense and you'll be okay.'

"She said that encounter helped her so much; not necessarily the words you said, but the fact that you took the time to listen to her. She told me that later, the words you'd said kicked in and pointed her back to her own wisdom; but at that moment in time, it was simply the fact that you listened."

"I didn't know that," Derek said. "I don't even remember that happening. I do know that when I've felt stressed and someone has taken the time to listen to me, I have felt the value of that listening. I don't mean just listening to my complaints and agreeing with me, but listening with compassion and neutrality, so that my complaints seem to melt away.

"That quality of listening calms me down, even if it's just for a moment; and often, clarity comes, helping me see how to better handle the circumstances. At the very least, when a person listens in that considerate way, they aren't adding fuel to the fire by agreeing with my complaints of 'Ain't it awful!'"

We chuckled at Derek's comment; then he got thoughtful again, saying, "So how does one survive in stressful conditions?"

"It seems to me, Derek, you already know the answer to that question. The example I just shared with you about your impact on the supervisor tells me you are helping employee morale more than you realize. You are doing this naturally, just by being yourself, with your calm manner and the depth of your listening.

"I also noticed you did not include yourself when you mentioned the executive team was concerned about retaining their jobs. May I ask why that is?"

"That's a very interesting question, Elsie." There was a thoughtful pause, and then he continued. "It's true; I'm not really concerned about my job. I trust that whatever happens, I'll be okay. I can't explain it," Derek said, as if he was a bit bewildered himself by this statement.

"You're well on track, Derek. You truly inspire me, and I have no doubt you inspire many of those you work with. The only thing I'll add is this: I encourage you to continue to observe and acknowledge common sense and wisdom in yourself, in your team and in the executive team, just like you did with the supervisor in the hallway.

"This acknowledgement reinforces and sustains a healthy state of mind where you can thrive, no matter the surrounding environment. Respecting your wisdom brings forth a deep feeling of well-being because you are directly connected to your true nature, to your true self. It's as if you are living in a state of grace, where insights occur. Every time you have an insight, it produces better results across the board, enhancing your personal and work life.

"I'm not saying there won't continue to be challenges as time goes on, Derek, and I don't want to imply that your current situation is a piece of cake; nor do I take lightly the stress that the company and workforce are undergoing. I'm simply saying, I know the more we live in harmony with our true nature, the less the outer world of chaos affects us.

"Living this way provides a clear state of mind to come up with solutions and innovative ideas as your industry changes. You mentioned that, yourself, when you were telling me how helpful deep listening is, in calming oneself down. You said when you calmed down, clarity surfaced.

"The fact that you trust you'll be okay, no matter what, is also a powerful indication that you already are living more in harmony with your wisdom than you think you are."

With a deep intake of breath, Derek said in a soft tone, "I feel I've had a breath of fresh air. Thank you!"

"I thank you, Derek. As I said earlier, you've inspired me and helped reinforce what I know and feel."

Surviving or thriving? You tell me.

Feed Them Salt

"*B*ut how do we get there? How do we get to our innate mental health?" implored a young woman at a Three Principles retreat. "I'm trying so hard to understand, but I don't get it," she declared, an edge to her voice. "What are the techniques or steps to get to the innate mental health you're talking about?"

I understood her frustration, so similar to my own experience when I was first introduced to the Principles. Their simplicity overrode my intellect, adding to my confusion. I could see this young woman, wondering how to "get" it, was in the same boat.

I reiterated that Mind, the Universal power behind life; Consciousness, the ability to be aware of our experience and the fact that we create it; and Thought, the ability to create our reality via our thinking, are the pathway to our innate health, or wisdom. Still, the young woman struggled to understand.

"There is nothing we need to do to 'get' the Principles, for the simple reason that we already *are* the Principles in action," I pointed out. "The Principles are inherent in every human being. The harder we try, the more distant the Principles seem. The 'trying' erects a barrier to the natural resiliency of our innate wisdom. Have patience; listen to the stories that are being shared, and perhaps one of them will prompt an insight for you. An insight is a direct experience of your wisdom."

When I was invited to conduct a retreat in New Zealand, it brought many fresh occurrences my way. For the most part, the group was unfamiliar with the Three Principles understanding, and as the day progressed, they experienced some confusion, as well as curiosity. However, as I related examples of how I and others had changed, and the impact of our transformations on those around us, both at home and in the workplace, people's interest was aroused.

A pastor at the retreat told me the way he engaged people was to "feed them salt." Instantly, my curiosity was stirred and I queried him about his statement. "I tell stories that give people hope," he replied. "The stories are the salt. The stories make people thirsty for more knowledge and they listen more intently."

I loved his explanation, as that is something Syd consistently encouraged, right from the beginning, as he taught me and others how to share the Principles.

"Tell stories," he would insist. *"The stories are alive with feeling and the feeling will open people to their own wisdom."*

As my training opportunities advanced, I learned to value this simple and profound advice. When people listen attentively, they are being in the moment; being in the moment is an enjoyable, relaxing experience. As people relax, they find it is easy and natural to learn via insight. Because we have been conditioned to learn using our memory and intellect, learning through insight can throw us for a loop. Our educational system is primarily based on learning by study and repetition, by absorbing information through the intellect. This is fine, except when the intellectual process gets in the way of learning something deeper; something called innate wisdom.

At the retreat, the participants' intellects were running headlong into the unknown realm of wisdom. They had no signposts to guide them, other than feelings of curiosity and enjoyment. I knew that, as the two-day program progressed, these deeper feelings would help calm their minds, and open some people to new understanding. When they shared these insights, it would be beneficial to the group as a whole. It would show the value of letting one's thinking slow down enough to admit new information, from within one's own consciousness.

As I strolled along the beautiful white sand beach after the first day of the retreat, I noticed a playground above the shoreline, where a young father was tending his small child. I sat on a nearby stretch of lawn, leaned back against a tree, and observed the happy family. The wee tyke had barely learned to walk, tottering precariously on chubby legs. He fell on his well-padded bottom, squeezed his face up and howled his indignant protest. Dad patiently picked him up, dusted him off, and gave him a cuddle. He then put the child into a toddler size swing, and gently pushed him to and fro. Soon the little one had forgotten his tears and was chortling with glee; totally engrossed in the moment, living life to the fullest. The child and father were using the Three Principles in the healthiest manner, without even knowing it; naturally living a life of pure pleasure in that moment of time.

Noticing the family being so in-the-moment brought to mind my arrival in New Zealand, at 6 AM the previous Monday. My friends had met me at the airport at this early hour, and in my excitement at being in a new country, jet lag wasn't really an issue. Prior to my arrival, I had really wondered how jet lag would affect me. It was a 14 hour trip; leaving Vancouver to fly to Los Angeles, then 3 hours layover in LA prior to an all-night flight, without much sleep, to Auckland. I thought I would be a wreck. To my pleasant surprise, I felt quite well.

My friends drove me to a wonderful vantage point, high above the city, to see the fantastic view of the surrounding area; small islands placed here and there on the turquoise water, palm trees swaying gracefully in the breeze. It was an incredible start to my month long stay in New Zealand.

Once we arrived at my hosts' home and I had time to freshen up before a beautifully prepared breakfast, my friends asked if I would care to join them on their friends' yacht for a trip out in the bay, where we would anchor and have lunch. I thought

I heard my hosts say, "tomorrow" so I eagerly agreed, thinking this would give me time to rest before the cruise. I noticed my friends were rushing a bit through breakfast, but didn't think much about it until it was suggested I finish my coffee, as their friends would be waiting for us on the beach with a dinghy, to take us to the vessel, anchored offshore.

"I thought we were going out tomorrow!" I exclaimed.

I did a double take as I heard my friends say, "No, the invitation to cruise and have lunch is for today!"

Soon I found myself in the dinghy, motoring out to the impressive yacht. I clambered aboard, holding on to my straw hat and within moments, the captain pulled up anchor. We sped off, trailing a wake of white waves, leaving the shore behind. It was then I discovered that my jet lag had also been left behind! I'd forgotten about it, as I set out on this new adventure of seeing New Zealand from the sea. In my total enjoyment of the cruise, feeling the sea mist on my face, seeing the incredibly beautiful rolling hills of surrounding land, dotted with sheep and cattle, I was deeply moved. My hosts and their friends demonstrated the warm hospitality New Zealanders are famous for, which helped me feel right at home.

The whole experience of arriving in New Zealand, and my comfort level with whatever was going on, gave me a fresh appreciation for the power of being in the moment. Not just for the sheer enjoyment of "being" but for the inner clarity that came to me because my mind was so quiet. I had new insights that helped me understand certain situations that had been bothering me. Stress vanished. There was no room for stress in the moment.

Being in the moment was a topic that captured the interest of the group at the retreat. Some had difficulty relating to the power and value of insights, and understanding that insights occur when your mind is still. Yet on the second day of the retreat, as their minds got quieter, there were a number of people who realized that in the past, they'd had spontaneous creative ideas that were of great benefit. One manager, a marathon runner, recalled a time he was running and new ideas occurred to him for an article he was writing. He was quite taken with the idea that you can nurture a quiet, calm state of mind where insights happen more of the time.

That story brought out another example, from a woman executive who loved to swim. "I often think of solutions to problems when I'm swimming and I have nothing on my mind. The ideas just seem to pop into my head. But I never thought you could cultivate this process. Is this what you're talking about when you keep pointing us to our innate health? Is that where insights come from?" I suggested she wait and see if she could answer her own questions at the end of the retreat. She smiled and said, "I know the answer already."

One business leader, who had arrived the first day of the retreat with a tight face, stressed and uneasy, sloppily dressed, visibly underwent a transformation overnight. When he entered the room on the second day, we were all surprised at how his face and demeanor had changed. He was relaxed, loose, and at ease. He was wearing a smart looking shirt and trousers so that even his clothes reflected his new state of mind.

When asked what had happened, he seemed at a loss to articulate what he had learned. The most he could say was, "I realized my wife and I have experienced some of what you've been talking about, but I didn't know we all had innate health, that it is natural. For some reason, this has made a big difference to me. I feel I can count on this to help me when the going gets tough."

A management consultant had this realization. "I've been waiting for an insight to happen and really trying to be patient, but it wasn't working. It wasn't until I went for a walk on the beach, noticing the shells and enjoying being on my own for the first time in quite a while, that I had an insight. It surprised me, coming out of nowhere. I realized I've been too busy. I live two blocks from the sea and this is the first time in ages I've walked on the beach. I've been too busy to take time to enjoy life, and life has been passing me by.

"The insights I've been waiting for have also been passing me by—until I slowed down and enjoyed the moment. Then, without thinking or trying, insight happened. It is amazing to see that you really don't have to do anything to 'get' the Three Principles understanding. Just 'being' is enough. Just 'being' is like feeding people salt. It makes you thirsty for more!"

The retreat ended with people feeling thoughtful and reflective; some still not certain what they had learned, but glad to have had their minds aerated. One of the managers said, "At the very least, I am questioning my assumptions of how life works. I do see that I have been very set in my ways. But other than that, I don't know what I've gained."

There were a few chuckles, as many felt that for the manager to even question his beliefs showed courage and an open mind. At that point, wisdom is doing its' job, opening the door to new insights, making people thirsty for more.

Seeing Beyond the Words

*N*ew Zealand guide books refer to their country as the Creator's personal retreat, Godzone, or God's own country. Some think the expression is a little over the top, but as a first-time visitor to this incredible land, I found it truly wonderful and worthy of the term. I tried to capture the beauty with my digital camera and found I could not do it justice, so I simply enjoyed the stunning scenery with my eyes and stored the images in memory.

I saw mountains on the horizon, interspersed with emerald green, rolling hills, natural terraces worn into these steep knolls by countless generations of grazing cattle and sheep. I saw beautiful azure seas stretching out before me, and islands jutting up from the ocean. I was astonished by the diversity and abundance of flowers and plants; including roses, honeysuckle, hibiscus, bougainvillea, snail vine with its intoxicating fragrance, and so many other varieties, growing together in harmony. Vegetables were bursting with health, their color and flavor intense. Dairy products were rich and creamy, from contented, grass fed cows.

The glorious environment I was blessed to experience during my month long stay brought me a great deal of peace. I felt immersed in a fertile ambience conducive to insights. Everywhere I turned, an opportunity presented itself for me to *see* something new; to *see* more fully the spiritual nature of life and of humanity.

However, the assignment life provided for me didn't always fall into the pattern I expected.

The people I met at the two retreats I conducted in New Zealand were fascinating; very independent, opinionated, passionate about what they believed in, and warmly hospitable. Some were challenging in a respectful manner; not quick to jump on the bandwagon of new thinking, assessing new ideas with consideration. Nonetheless, when insights occurred during the course of the training, there was genuine acceptance of something new to discover, something new to learn, something beneficial.

The experiences I shared with the group I met at the first retreat are featured in the previous chapter, "Feed Them Salt." The group in the second retreat indicated a desire to go "deeper" into understanding the Three Principles. They had been learning about their inner wisdom for a while and many changes had taken place in their lives. Now they were eager for more.

I also was keen to meet the group and to go "deeper." After preliminary introductions were made and I had welcomed the group, I was ready to go. What transpired next was an incredible opportunity to *see* beyond words, to walk my talk. An interesting situation began to unfold.

In my anticipation of "deeper," I had gotten caught up in my personal thinking of what I considered "deeper" to mean— talking about the nature of the Principles and so on. I didn't hear that the audience was more curious about "packaging" the Principles than learning about the nature of the Principles, so I side-stepped their requests to talk about this subject. Not *hearing* them, I felt the topic was irrelevant to going deeper. I let them know that as they gained more understanding, they would realize it was unnecessary to package the Principles. "You'll see," I responded, "that you cannot package the Principles because they are formless Energy."

This is true; you cannot package the Principles; you lose the very essence, that deep feeling, if you intellectualize them. However, the fact was that, not being in the moment, and caught up in my thinking, I wasn't attentive to the needs of the group. This was creating a situation where no one was listening, including me. Rather than listening, I was focused more on my need to go deeper, in my way. Thank goodness for the power of insight, as you will see.

Several in the group persisted in exploring the idea of having some sort of structure around the Principles in order to make them more comprehensible to their clients, colleagues, employees and so on; I felt the real issue here was that they wanted a structure to help better understand the Principles themselves— that this was their way of going "deeper."

Still rummaging around in my belief system, I didn't see how pertinent the topic of "packaging" was. I had a few moments of frustration in wanting to move past this theme. The feeling of frustration alerted me to the fact that I had an expectation of how the program should go; it dawned on me that the expectation was getting in the way of my listening to the group. All at once, everything became clear. It took an insight to turn my inner hearing on, so I could *hear* that they needed to have some relevance. The topic they were curious about was a perfect teaching point to explore the relevance of the Principles to everything in life, including "packaging" the Principles.

As insight cleared my mind and brought me into the moment, I addressed the group. "Let me start again," I began. "I realize I haven't fully listened to you, and I apologize. Something just occurred to me that I'd like to run by you. See if this makes sense."

Now I had everyone's attention. "What occurred to me was that when you say 'structure,' you are simply looking for a way to help others see how the Principles have relevance to people's lives. Is that right?"

"What do you mean by relevance?" someone asked.

"Connecting something that is important to those you are speaking with to the new information you want to introduce," I replied. "By making a connection between something familiar to the group, i.e. structure, with something that is unfamiliar, i.e. the Principles, you bridge the gap between the known and unknown."

They pondered this idea for a moment, and then I saw faces light up as excitement ignited the participants. Several people really clicked to the idea of relevance and all of a sudden, insights emerged from them about how to enhance their services to clients and colleagues.

They saw that the first thing they needed to do was to be in the moment as much as possible, allowing them to listen more deeply to their clients to assess their needs. They discerned that their ability to listen deeply would bring out the necessary information needed to connect and provide relevance to the Principles; to help guide people in a healthy direction.

They pointed out that when I had regrouped mentally in order to *listen* to them, without my personal thinking acting as a barrier, they were able to hear me better; they saw how important being in the moment is to having a clear state of mind, and to *seeing* beyond the words.

As these thoughts emerged in our group, one individual remarked, "It seems to me, while we were trying to go deeper, this prevented us from doing so. Once we stopped trying, the deepening of our understanding happened naturally." We all agreed. It was obvious that our mental and spiritual understanding of how the Principles operate, as well as understanding what the Principles are, had definitely evolved. We had all become more aware that we are the Principles in action.

I was very appreciative of their insightful comments regarding being in the moment, *seeing* beyond the words, and the remark that "trying" to go deeper, in essence, prevented us from doing so. All in all, I felt elevated by their observations and knew they had taught me as much as I had shared with them, if not more. A thought whispered in my mind that my ability to be more in the moment had taken a big leap during this training.

The notion of seeing beyond time, space and matter, an insight by Sydney Banks, has always intrigued me but was totally beyond my comprehension. For the first time, in New Zealand, I began to get a feeling that when I was in the moment, just "being," this feeling was a tiny glimmer beyond time, space and matter.

The feeling felt natural and I found a deeper peace and contentment in my own company. The feeling was coming from within me, not because of anything; it just was.

There was a timeless moment of lying on the beach and feeling my bones melt into the sand. Utter peace descended upon me. Then I heard a dog bark and sat up, observing the animal frolicking on the shore. With a sudden burst of speed, it bounded after some seagulls as they flew out of reach. Undeterred, the dog suddenly changed direction, leaping toward his master, who was calling him to heel. Off they wandered, in their own world, content to be together.

Another timeless moment in New Zealand: I attended, with friends, an outdoor concert, "A Carnival of Music—With the Stars Under the Stars" featuring Dame Malvina Major. As Cultural Ambassador, she has performed at many New Zealand Embassies throughout the world, and was named New Zealand Entertainer of the year in 1992.

It was a casual affair starting in the late afternoon, people bringing picnic baskets or dinner boxes to enjoy. Some were reclining on blankets, others lounging comfortably in canvas camping chairs. There was an air of excitement as people greeted one another, visiting groups here and there. Soon the sky darkened and we were entertained by first class performers.

It was a spellbinding evening and as we wound our way home, my host and hostess pulled over and drove up a dark rural road so I could see the Southern Cross. We emerged from the car, under a black velvet sky sparkling with diamonds. A night owl hooted, welcoming us to his territory. The Milky Way formed a pathway across part of the sky—so dense you felt you could reach up and touch it. Sighting the Southern Cross, the four points clearly identified, brought an end to our magical evening.

The feeling of timelessness lingered throughout my stay in God's country. I know this feeling of "*being* in the moment" is readily available to all. God's country exists inside each and every one of us; it is our birthright.

Part Three

The Principles
in
Personal Relationships

Roller Coaster Ride

The last couple of months had been an interesting time, with emotions peaking and ebbing; similar to the way one's stomach feels on the ups and downs of a roller coaster ride. As I've said before, I've never enjoyed roller coasters! However I must say that the learning gained, spiritually and mentally, made the emotional ride worthwhile.

To begin with, I'd taken some time off, except for a few coaching calls with long term clients. This was a welcome respite after a busy year, journeying to various training locations throughout the States and New Zealand. As much as I enjoyed the adventure of sharing the Three Principles, I found myself needing a rest. Still, it took a bit of adjusting to really relax. My tired state of mind brought out my old insecurities. Guilt was a factor—did I deserve to take all that time off? Was I letting my clients down? Would I forget what I had learned? Would I lose my competency and be left behind by other practitioners?

Foolish questions, weren't they? Yet in a moment of insecurity, guilt reared its ugly head and ego superseded wisdom for a time; happily, not for long. As I moved past my uncertainty, I relished the time I had with my husband, Ken, and enjoyed our garden and home like never before. My mind filled with beauty and peace, cosmic humor came into play and life became an absolute pleasure. Being with family and friends took on new meaning, imbued with more love.

During this time, because of medical issues, Ken contemplated taking early retirement from his woodworking job. We discussed the idea at length; Ken researched the financial numbers and decided he would make the leap. At first, everything seemed to flow and we were elated at the prospect of having more time together; to travel, to leisurely beautify our retirement home, and simply to enjoy life.

Then several unexpected issues cropped up that put a damper on our elation. In order for Ken to receive his pension from the United States, where we had resided for almost two decades, he would have to resign from our Principles based business, where he handled the accounting and so on, and could no longer work for the company, even part time. It took a while for the information to penetrate my happiness. Finally the penny dropped, and both Ken and I took a dip on the roller coaster. What a ride! Way down! It took the heat of a couple of negative interactions between us before we realized this mental arena was not where we wanted to be.

Then common sense took over; we approached our accountant and came up with solutions to the matters before us. There is nothing quite like a dip south to wake up the senses, to re-engage the soul and to make one grateful for understanding that we have the ability to create experience. I hate to think how long we might have lingered in mental distress, had we not had some understanding. We could have ended up deciding that Ken should delay his retirement, and spoil what was to become a highlight of our life together—the gateway to our "golden years."

I was hesitant to relate the following story to you; but after discussing this with Ken and receiving his permission, we both felt it was important to share. Many "baby boomers" are going through similar situations with their parents, and may find our experience helpful.

Ken's mother, at the age of ninety-four years, was in need of more care and attention. She called herself a "free spirit" and we agreed with her. She was frail, used a cane and walker, but was a feisty, independent thinker. Mom was unaware that she needed more care. She had Vascular Dementia and her cognition was limited.

For a number of years, Mom had being lovingly cared for by her daughter and son-in-law. When we moved back to Salt Spring from California, Ken was able to add his support and take on some of the responsibility. But there came a point when Mom needed additional care and it was necessary to move her into an assisted living residence on Vancouver Island. This worked well for a while.

After many incidents of wandering away from her lodgings, forgetting where she lived, and being brought back by some kind soul, the straw that broke the camel's back was when Mom was escorted back to her quarters by two young police officers. Mom quite enjoyed the ride in the police car and the attention, until she received a scolding from the staff. She told them in no uncertain terms, "I am a free spirit and will go for a walk if I want to!"

The staff let us know it was time to make plans for moving Mom to a secure facility where she would no longer have the freedom to leave without someone accompanying her. It was too dangerous for her to go out on her own, in case she fell and broke a hip bone or whatever. We were told she needed twenty-four hour attention.

After conferring with Ken's sister, we let Mom know we were researching various care homes in different areas; at one point, we made an appointment to view a suite in a senior's residence, but at the last minute, Mom refused to go.

As we continued our search, we were delighted to find an elder care residence close to us, on Salt Spring Island. We felt this would be the perfect place for Mom. We could pop in and visit, have her over for dinner, and take her for rides around our beautiful area. It seemed an answer to all our prayers.

After making arrangements with the facility, we were given advice on how to share this new information with Mom. We were told that at her age and with her limited cognition, change of any sort is very frightening. It was suggested that we drive her to her new home, and then tell her about the change. This didn't feel right to Ken and me. We decided to play things by ear and be in the moment as much as possible.

The day came to take Mom to her new home. After talking with the staff where she was living at the time, we found Mom finishing her breakfast, enjoying a last cup of coffee, surrounded by her table mates. Ken and I looked at one another; should we wait till she was alone or jump right in?

Ken started the ball rolling by letting her know we had come to take her to Salt Spring, that we had found an intermediate care facility close to us. We described the beautiful gardens surrounding her new residence, and shared our delight that she would be close to us. She took us totally by surprise, saying, "You've made me the happiest woman on earth. When do we leave?"

We picked up a few items Mom would need, gave her time to say good-bye to her friends, and then off we went. We would come back another day to clean up the rest of her suite and collect some of her precious mementos to help her feel more comfortable in her new room. Mom was ecstatic to be moving close to us, and we were relieved at the gentleness of this transition. She did not question us then or later about her things and what we should do with them. The matter was not in her world and was left for us to deal with.

When we brought her into her new home, she was fine. We introduced her to the staff, and had lunch with her in the dining room. She wasn't paying attention to the other residents until we took her into the lounge. Some were dozing peacefully in their chairs, while others looked like they were in another world. Mom started to get quiet and we could feel her beginning to get stressed. The staff recommended we take her to her room and leave her to rest for a couple of hours. It was like leaving your child at kindergarten, when she is doubtful about staying. It was very difficult.

When we went back that evening, her state of mind had changed; she was furious with us. She berated us for leaving her there and indignantly told us she would not stay in this place. We did our best to calm her down; assuring her she would find new friends because she was such a social person. This made no difference to her. We sat with Mom for a while as she continued to vent, then hugged her, and let her know we were just minutes away and would be back in the morning.

Mom was in no better spirits the next day, and poured out her misery. We did not take her behavior personally, knowing she was responding out of fear. It had dawned on us that when we said we were bringing her to Salt Spring, she thought she was coming to live with us. With her lack of cognition, she didn't hear what we had really said; that we were moving her close to us.

We continued to respond to her with love, and pointed out the advantages of being near us so we could see her more often. Ken told her the facility was highly rated for the care they provided. We acknowledged that it was not easy or pleasant seeing how dazed some of the residents were, but also pointed out that they seemed at peace, and that the staff was kind and patient.

Just then, one of the woman residents sitting at another table came up to Mom and patted her on the shoulder, saying, "My name is Ellen. This is really quite a nice place. You'll like it. The food is great, the gardens are beautiful, and the staff is wonderful. If you want to talk, just come to me." Both Ken and I were so touched by her kindness. Mom acknowledged Ellen with a shaky smile.

We were told by the staff, and also found information in the booklet given to us, about the phases of change and length of time this type of transition would take. The booklet said it could take anywhere from four to six weeks, and in some cases, up to six months for residents to adjust to their new surroundings. Ken and I read the document but did not buy into the categorization. Intuitively, we felt if we consistently looked to Mom's innate mental health rather than categorize her behavior, there would be better results. We focused on positivity because it felt better, for Mom and for us.

Mom basically adjusted in three days. On the third day, when we went to visit her, she embraced us, telling us how happy she was to see us. As we walked by some residents on our way to the gardens, we passed one senior who was sitting staring into space; Mom commented with compassion, "Poor soul."

In three days, her state of mind had moved from anger, feelings of betrayal, fear and resistance, to compassion. Certainly, she went in and out of moods during her time there; there were days when she would greet us with complaints and the desire to 'break out of here,' but overall, her adjustment didn't take as long as predicted. Unconditional love helped Mom adjust, I have no doubt.

Mom had always been rather strong minded, but in the first stages of the disease, without her knowing why, she became fearful and paranoid; as a result, her negativity increased. We were told this was a symptom of the illness.

As the illness progressed, and her brain functions and synapses deteriorated, her negativity lessened. This amazed us. She became more loving as her cognition decreased, taking away her more recent memories. Childhood memories were more positive and she regaled us with fond stories from that era. She lived in a world of her own making, most of it positive and enjoyable. She took absolute delight in our car rides, loved nature, and adored dessert! There was a childlike quality about her reality, an unself-consciousness that was endearing to us.

Mom's journey on this earth ended two years later. Even at the very end of her time, when she had two percent brain function left, we knew she felt our presence, although she didn't acknowledge it verbally or visually. Holding her hand was enough; the human touch brought solace.

I would never have thought there was anything positive about Mom's condition; but seeing is believing. We saw there was something that transcended the physical functions of the brain; the spiritual essence of each and every human being.

Wisdom Never Sleeps

*A*s I went for my morning walk, enjoying the crunch of newly fallen snow underfoot, my thoughts meandered lazily. It came to mind that just as nature has seasons—spring, summer, fall and winter—so do human beings.

I wondered why human souls fall asleep. Why don't we continue to grow at a nice steady pace, gaining new inner knowledge that guides our lives forward, with more well-being? It sounds like I'm asking a lot, I know. I can't say that I came up with an answer. It seems it just is.

In nature, a dormant period is required for plants and some animals to rest. In the spring, as the weather warms, seeds sprout and grow; animals awaken from hibernation, hungry for food. Perhaps there is some parallel in humans; a period of rest, then upon awakening once again, a time of hunger for new inner knowledge to feed the soul.

It has become apparent to me that wisdom never sleeps. Our mental and spiritual understanding may slumber for a time; but underneath, deep within, wisdom is alive and well, always waiting to be released.

Our ego plays a big part in hindering the process of inner growth. What's so amazing and humorous about this statement is that ego is really an illusion, made up of our thoughts about who we are. Our ego is what we think of as our personal identity, and depends on what we've accomplished; an image of self-importance.

Thoughts create feelings; if we harbor thoughts of ambition, competition, jealousy, envy and so on, we will be filled with corresponding feelings. This is not a place I care to live in, although it is a place I am familiar with.

Consciousness, intertwined with Mind, guides us to the awareness that our free will can use the neutral power of Thought to create any experience—positive or negative, healthy or unhealthy. This knowledge informs our decisions, helping us to make wiser choices; to "think healthier." Instead of being a victim of circumstances, we realize we always have a choice. *Knowing* we have a choice brings clarity and stops us from hibernating in old patterns of thought.

Beyond ego lies our true identity, source of inner wisdom, a natural expression of Universal Mind. Even when our ego seems in control, deep within us is a *knowing* that we have fallen into a pit of our own making. An illusionary pit, to be sure; but because we use thought to create our experience, the pit can feel very, very real.

Is this knowledge helpful? I would say, very much so. At the least, it prevents us from wallowing in our misery for too long. The best thing about knowing wisdom never sleeps is that you always get a second chance. If you have the honesty and humility to acknowledge that you've been sleeping, that your growth has become static; then once again—miraculously it seems—you continue your inner journey.

As I walked along, I recalled a time when my learning had plateaued. I was barely conscious of a feeling of staleness; my life and work were okay, but I didn't feel a great deal of energy; I had a sense of "been there, done that."

One evening, when Ken and I were having dinner out with Syd, he mentioned an upcoming conference he was giving. I was aware of the event, and let Syd know I didn't think we would be able to attend this time, due to other commitments. This was during the period of settling Ken's mother in her elder care facility, so in my mind, the reason we weren't going was justified. I didn't allow myself to consider that I was holding back from learning more.

Over the years, Ken and I had attended almost every event where Syd spoke, so not going to this one was very unusual. Ken said, "You can go, Elsie. I'll stay with Mom to make sure she's okay." I felt uncomfortable, but didn't want to look at my discomfort, so I continued to make excuses.

Syd spoke softly, *"This will be my last seminar, Elsie."*

Chuckling, I teased Syd that I had heard that comment from him before. It was true; he'd said many times over the years that an upcoming talk would be his "last conference."

Not another word did he speak about my attending the event. He was very kind to me that evening; it was as if he were caring for someone in ill health.

When Ken and I got home later that evening, I was very agitated. Over and over again, I rationalized in my mind the logic for not going to the seminar. Ken remained quiet, other than to say once more, "You can go, Elsie, if you want to." I had a very restless sleep that night.

The next day, Ken and I were having coffee at a local café. While we were there, we happened to meet two longtime friends who joined us at our table. Our friends spoke about gratitude and keeping the feeling alive. I felt their words were aimed directly at me and was very uncomfortable. We didn't linger over coffee but hastened home.

Continuing to mull over the conversation with our friends, I heard the phone ring. I picked it up and another friend said, "I hear you're not going to the conference, Elsie. I'm going to miss you. This will be the first time you've not been there."

I was fired up by her words, and retorted, "Did Syd ask you to call me?" I figured for sure, he must have called her and asked her to talk with me. In surprise, she responded, "No, Elsie; I've not spoken to him. I just wanted to tell you I'll miss your presence. I'd love to see you."

Chastened by her genuineness and love, I realized I was in a mire of my own creation. In a flash of clarity, I knew I had to go to Syd's talk. Thanking my friend for her call, I hung up the phone, went into Ken's office, and said, "Hon, I'm going to Syd's conference." He smiled affectionately, "Go for it, darling. I'm glad. It's right you should be there."

In a matter of minutes, I'd arranged for my flight, booked my accommodations, and was set to go. I felt elevated by my decision; at the same time, I felt humbled by my experience. I knew I had to go; I had been hibernating too long.

When I saw Syd the first morning of the conference, he embraced me and told me he was very pleased to see me. I could feel his gentle, unconditional love.

As it turned out, this was Syd's last conference. I'll never forget his kindness, his love and support; nor will I ever forget the gentle encouragement from Ken, from the wise, loving friends we'd met at the café, or from the dear friend who called to share her love. This experience was life-changing for me. It softened me, and opened up my mind to see that we never stop learning; that wisdom never sleeps, even though we do.

When we move out of slumber and forward into new learning, it's as if our mental landscape has been gentled, made more malleable so that seeds of insight burst into the open and then flower.

As my walk progressed and the sun rose overhead, the snow began to melt. Drops of water fell lightly from cedar boughs as I walked beneath them. Patches of meadow lay exposed to the clear blue sky.

In like manner, the warmth of wisdom melts the confining patterns of thought, revealing clarity of mind. A feeling of gratitude swept through me as I continued my journey. Indeed, wisdom resides deep within, waiting for the ego to thaw and innate wisdom to manifest.

The roots of knowledge are deep and provide stability. These strong roots allow us to be buffeted by the winds of change, *knowing* we will be okay as long as we stick to the fundamentals of who and what we really are. If we can see the human spirit is connected to Universal Mind, to wisdom, I *know* we won't lose our way.

Mining for Treasure

*W*hen individuals are gripped by despair, sorrow, anger, bitterness or other unhelpful emotions, it can be difficult for them to even consider that beneath their gloomy perspective resides inherent common sense. Yet, if you listen carefully to their conversation, you will find un-mined treasure of which they may be totally unaware. Then you can, when appropriate, direct them to their own inner resources.

In summertime, you may have occasionally noticed a beachcomber sweeping a metal detector across the sand, looking for lost gold, rings, coins, or other treasures. Listening for people's innate wisdom is like using a mental health detector; you will always find some gold nuggets, if you listen deeply enough.

Let me share a story about Glen and Nina, a retired couple, married many years. The death of their only son at the age of twenty-five had devastated them. For months, they remained inconsolable. Glen, in utter despair, contemplated suicide. His wife, who was going through her own anguish, was deeply concerned about her husband; she loved and comforted him the best she could.

The couple's close friend, Alan, staunchly supported them both, listened to their heartache, and assisted where possible. At some point, Alan gave them Sydney Banks' book, *The Enlightened Gardener*, which helped them calm down. Still, the father struggled with his desolation, and felt his life was over.

Alan asked Glen what he had found helpful in Syd's book. "It's a nice book, Alan, and it has some interesting theories, but it didn't really speak to my reality. I've lost my son and nothing is going to bring him back. That's reality," replied Glen, in a lackluster tone.

"I know nothing will bring back your son, Glen. I don't pretend to know what you're feeling because I've never lost a child. My heart goes out to you," Alan said earnestly. "You're my buddy, and I hate to see you suffering. Is there anything I can do for you?"

"Nobody can do anything for me. My life is meaningless," Glen responded despairingly.

"Don't talk that way, Glen," Alan said forcefully. "What about the love and support of your wife and relatives?"

"Yeah, I know. Nina has been incredible throughout this tragedy. She has a quiet strength that keeps her going, and her patient understanding has been helpful to me when I've been at my lowest point. But I'm not like her. I don't have anything I can count on now that my son is gone."

"The fact that you can see and feel Nina's quiet strength tells me there's something in you that resonates with her inner power; that power has touched and helped you."

"Nonsense," protested Glen vehemently. "It's not about me; I've got nothing left inside—it's about Nina's strength, not mine. That's what helping me, sometimes."

"You've still got a choice, Glen, whether you choose to engage your strength or not. I see you use that power occasionally; my observation is when you do, you feel better," Alan said matter-of-factly.

"It's simply a momentary distraction from my pain; then I start to think of my son again and I'm lost. Please, Alan, I know you're trying to help, but let's stop talking about this now. I need a break," Glen cried out, holding his head in his hands, as if he couldn't bear to hear any more.

Alan wrapped his arm around Glen's shoulders and just held him quietly for a moment. "You got it, buddy. Look, I'm heading out to the lake this afternoon to do some trout fishing. Do you want to come along?"

There was a long pause then Glen said half-heartedly, "Sure; why not. It'll be a diversion for a while."

The longtime friends spent a quiet afternoon, leisurely rowing the boat around the lake; they caught and released a few trout. Not much conversation took place, and a feeling of peace stole over them as they drifted along in their craft. As dusk began to fall, subtle shades of mauve, blue, and rose tinged the soft gray sky, creating a mystical reflection on the surface of the lake. A loon's haunting call to his mate completed the scene. It was a magical moment, when all was perfection.

On the ride home, Glen told Alan how much he appreciated his friend's support for him and his wife in their time of grief. "Sometimes I feel as if I'm never going to come out of this grieving process, Alan, and I feel guilty if I start to enjoy myself. How can I be so hard-hearted to enjoy my life when my son is gone?" he asked gravely.

"What I see is that your common sense is moving you forward in life, Glen. Enjoying life is normal; it's our birthright. Nothing stays static, not even grief; everyone has their own pace with moving on. You take all the time you need to grieve, but please; trust your common sense." Alan said with passion. "Your son would want you to enjoy your life. You know that, Glen. Your son loved his life and enjoyed every moment."

They rode in silence for a time; then Alan softly offered, "You'll always have memories of your son. They'll never go away. Your son is still with you in your heart and soul."

"But it hurts to remember him, Alan, even the good times. It hurts because he's no longer with us. I don't know how I can get past that," Glen said solemnly.

"Is that state of mind where you want to live?"

"No!" Glen retorted adamantly. "I just don't know how to move on."

"You did move on; while we were on the lake, I could see the peace on your face. It's the most relaxed I've seen you in a long time. So that space is inside you already, otherwise you couldn't have felt it."

"Maybe," Glen responded.

"What do you do when you're on your own that brings peace of mind?"

"I don't know that what I experience could be called 'peace of mind,' but physical exercise seems to help, so I walk a lot. I also write now and then; I've started an article on fly fishing techniques. It's difficult to focus on my writing, but sometimes I get going and accomplish a few pages. It takes my mind off my grief. But really; all that is merely a diversion. It doesn't last long, and then my despair is back."

"What prompted you to write an article on fly fishing?"

"I don't know," Glen retorted, shrugging his shoulders. "It was just something to do; creating a distraction."

"I think that's terrific. It's your innate common sense moving you forward."

"No, it's just my survival instinct."

Alan burst out laughing, and shaking his head, said, "You're a tough nut to crack, my friend. Call it whatever you want. You're still doing some constructive things that are helping you move to a more accepting, peaceful state of mind."

"I don't know about that but I'm not going to argue with you. Nina is volunteering at the Homeless Shelter, helping dish out lunch, and that's providing some solace for her. But she's still really struggling."

"You both have a lot of courage, Glen. To be in service to others—whether its tips on fly fishing, or helping feed the homeless—it's all beneficial, for you and for them."

"Well, I'm not getting my hopes up. You're too optimistic, Alan, but you're a good friend, and I know you're genuinely trying to help us."

"All I ask is that you give yourself some credit for your own wisdom in doing what you're doing; call it survival instinct or common sense. You're discovering hidden treasures inside of yourself."

"Oh, don't go all poetic on me," Glen replied with a wry grin.

After Alan dropped Glen off, he continued his drive home, and reflected how helpful it was to be "normal" with Glen, spending a quiet afternoon fishing together instead of trying to turn Glen away from his unhelpful emotions. Experiencing a healthy time together was far more powerful than talking about how thought creates experience.

It was "living in a healthy feeling" rather than "talking about a healthy feeling" that brought relief to them both. The positive experience provided Glen with some respite from his negative thoughts. Taking the attention off negative thoughts allowed the natural healthy default setting to emerge. Alan conceded to himself that there was a place for education—describing how humans create their own experience—as well as living in well-being. Clearly, the partnership between education and experience was a powerful force. The old saying, "lead by example" had never been so meaningful to Alan.

Several days later, Alan and his girlfriend, Marisa, joined Glen and Nina for a hike through a regional park. There were many trails to choose from and the couples decided on the coastal trail, overlooking magnificent views of the ocean. After a brisk hour long walk, they found a comfortable spot on a sunny patch of grass, sat down, and pulled out their lunch and drinks. Munching their sandwiches, they observed a squirrel darting between the trees, busily gathering fallen nuts. With bulging cheeks, the squirrel scampered up the tree with its treasure, noisily chattering away.

The couples remarked on the industrious nature of the squirrel, and Glen said how much his son would have enjoyed this outing. The mood turned pensive, and Glen began to bring out his usual remarks about the loss of his son. Alan and Marisa glanced at each other, uncertain what to do, other than listen.

As the mood continued to deteriorate, Alan was just about to suggest they continue their walk when Nina spoke softly. "That's enough, Glen; I refuse to listen anymore to how awful the loss of our son is. You always talk about the loss of your son, but he was my son too."

Glen's face had a chagrined look as he said, "I can't let it go, Nina. The reality is we'll never see our son again and—"

Nina interrupted Glen. Looking straight into his eyes, her words seeming to pierce through to his very soul, she passionately said, "I don't want to hear it, Glen. I want to remember our son with love. He was an affectionate, kind-hearted soul, seeing the best in everyone. Do you think he would want us to remain in misery?"

There was a long, drawn-out silence; then Glen said quietly, "No, he wouldn't, Nina. You're right. My mind has been filled with so much thinking that I haven't been able to really listen to anyone."

The group somberly gathered their things together and backtracked to the car. When they reached the vehicle, Glen apologized to Alan and Marisa. "I know I haven't been great company, but I do appreciate you both spending time with us. It's very kind of you."

Turning to Nina, he wrapped his arms around her and quietly held her. "Thank you," he whispered.

After dropping the couple at their home, Alan and Marisa continued on their way. "When Nina spoke to Glen at the park, I sensed a turning point," Marisa said. "I don't know them as well as you do, Alan, but it certainly felt like something shifted for them. His face looked more relaxed on the way back from the park, as did Nina's. When they were walking up the path to their front door, Glen reached out for Nina's hand."

"Yes, I noticed that; I thought it was amazing how Nina spoke to Glen, with such love and understanding; at the same time, making it clear she'd had enough. It was humbling to witness that depth of honesty and emotion."

A few days later, Alan called Glen, "How are you, old buddy?" They carried on a conversation for a time; then Alan remarked that Glen sounded in better spirits.

"No, I'm not really. I'm the same. It's just that Nina won't let me get away with too much anymore. I don't know what's come over her. I think she's been reading those books you gave her from Sydney Banks. . . Thanks a lot," he said in an injured tone, then burst out laughing.

"Well, whatever is happening with the two of you, you sure sound good. Your sense of humor has returned."

"Seriously, I owe you a lot, Alan, for all your patience and kindness. The day we went fishing was very helpful to me. I slipped into 'normality' for a brief time, and it helped rest my mind. You're a good friend. I know I'll never forget my son, and the grief may come and go; but I've got to move on and live life. I'm starting to see I'm dishonoring my son by holding onto the sorrow, rather than celebrating the time we had with him."

From the calm conviction with which Glen said those words, Alan knew his friend was experiencing more tranquility. Filled with compassion and respect for the courage of the couple as they progressed on their inner journey, Alan felt at peace.

This is a powerful example of the influence, as Alan states, of "living in a healthy feeling" rather than "talking about a healthy feeling." This influence, coupled with Nina's wise position on how she wanted to remember her son with love, not sorrow, had helped both of them begin to live in a healthier reality.

Undoubtedly, there would be more for Glen and Nina to learn; but they had a much more solid foundation on which to build their future. Indeed, they had found, and had started to mine, the treasure within.

Emotions Are Ageless

I've discovered that emotions aren't equated to age; whether you are six or sixty, you can experience similar emotions. I used to think that as you got older, you would become wiser, and therefore more in control of your feelings. But that isn't necessarily the case, as you will see.

The way I view it, understanding emotions is about recognizing where they come from, rather than trying to control them; it is about discernment as opposed to will power. Realizing that we use Thought to create feelings brings great relief from mental stress. It puts the game of life in our court; in other words, the power to change resides in understanding the role of Thought. Unfortunately, many people don't know this, and innocently use their thoughts against themselves. They are, in a sense, victimized by their own thinking.

Many individuals hold habits of thought that distress them. If you don't know you are the thinker of those thoughts, and continue to entertain them, you are your own worst enemy. The following example, focusing on adults and seniors, illustrates this point.

Harriet, a feisty widow, was sixty-nine years old, and had been semi-estranged from her son, Wally, for several years. Harriet was quite judgmental and rigid in her beliefs about how she should be treated. She felt abandoned by her son because he seldom called; in her mind, this looked like he didn't care about her. They'd not had a specific falling out, rather a general pulling back from each other.

Harriet's son would dutifully call her on Mother's Day, on her birthday, and other special holidays. The calls were superficial and awkward. Neither felt good about them, nor saw how to move past the tension in their relationship.

Wally, in his early forties, was happily married and had a nice life with his wife. The only fly in the ointment, as far as Wally was concerned, was his mother. He knew he was neglectful, but simply couldn't abide any more stressful conversations with her. His mother was always in the back of his mind, but he just didn't have the heart to call her more often and face another uncomfortable exchange.

Harriet was sure the situation was her son's fault. She felt he should have more respect for her—after all, she reasoned, she was pregnant with him for nine long months, and took care of him from infancy through early adulthood. As she saw it, she worked her fingers to the bone for him.

Wally's perspective was that his mother was too set in her ways. He did love her, but didn't want to get into any more confrontations; so he dealt with the situation by avoiding her as much as possible. He didn't feel good about this.

Finally, the state of affairs came to a head. Harriet was about to turn seventy. Her son was fully aware of this, but hadn't planned anything to celebrate her birthday. Wally's sister, Wilma, had a healthy relationship with her mother; she called Wally and suggested they take Harriet out for a special luncheon, just the three of them, without their families. "It'll be like the old days," Wilma said, "when we three had fun together. What'd you say?" Wally half-heartedly agreed, and Wilma offered to set it up.

Without wasting any time, Wilma placed the call to her mother. They caught up on the neighborhood gossip; then Wilma brought up the birthday outing. "I've been talking with

Wally, and we'd love to take you out for a special birthday lunch. Is there any place in particular you'd like to go?"

"Wally hasn't said anything to me about this," Harriet replied in a fretful tone. "He never calls, and never invites me anywhere, so why now?"

Wilma tried to smooth things over, but her mother resisted. As Harriet brought up all the things she felt were wrong with her son, Wilma could hear the strain in her voice. She realized that although Harriet had covered up much of her hurt over the last few years, as soon as she talked about it, the pain returned.

The daughter was surprised at how emotional her mother had become. She was well aware of the difficult relationship between mother and son; after trying many times to bring some harmony to the situation, she had decided it was best to leave them to sort it out. Whenever she tried to help them resolve their differences, they both got upset with her.

It dawned on Wilma that her mother was creating her own emotional pain by her negative thinking; however, she felt this wasn't a good time to point out that fact. Perhaps an indirect approach would be better in this situation. Driving her decision was the familiar adage: "Nothing ventured—nothing gained."

"Mom, you know Wally loves you. He just doesn't want to argue with you, so he stays away. When he does call, the tone of the conversation upsets him. He feels insecure with you; like he's not loved and accepted for who he is. He's really stressed out about this."

"Well, I'm stressed out too!" Harried replied emphatically. "And I don't feel loved either; I don't know if I want to go to lunch with him. The awkwardness will just start up all over again."

Wilma could feel her mother getting more agitated, and wanted to calm her down. "Look, Mom," she said in a conciliatory tone, "you both feel the same, but I know Wally wants to be with you for your birthday. He loves you, Mom," Wilma repeated tenderly.

"If it's okay with you, I'd like to talk with Wally about how you're feeling. . . unless you'd rather have a heart-to-heart conversation with him yourself?"

"No," Harriet quickly replied. "Maybe if it comes from you, he'll hear it differently."

Wilma knew she was getting in the middle again; but for some reason, she felt more hopeful that this time her family might move toward a healthier relationship.

Cautiously optimistic, she called her brother. "Hi Wally; I spoke to Mom about her birthday luncheon. She's feeling a little doubtful that you really see this outing as a nice family celebration."

Wilma paused for a moment as she gathered her thoughts. "As I talked with each of you, it seemed to me you both have experienced many of the same emotions and stress because of the way you're thinking about each other. She's really hurting."

"Well, I'm hurting too, Wilma," her brother informed her curtly. Then he slowly added, "But I didn't know Mom was taking things so badly; I certainly don't like to think of her suffering. I just don't want to get into the same old conversation again."

"You don't have to talk about the past, Wally. Just let it be. Love dissolves the past. See her as your mother who is trying her best, given how she thinks about life. She loves you; I know she does. She just doesn't know how to express it. One of you has to put out a hand to the other."

Nothing was said for a few moments, then Wilma gently probed, "Do you want to have a better relationship with Mom?"

"Yes, of course I do," Wally responded testily. "I don't know if she does, though. I've tried in the past and it hasn't worked. What'll be different now?"

"I don't know, Wally. You can only try again. I do know that if your heart is in the right place, you won't take the things she says so personally. Maybe if you don't get upset with her, she'll back off."

"Let me think about it," Wally responded in a low tone.

That evening, Wilma was talking to her husband about her conversations with Harriet and Wally. "They're both in mental pain from their negative thoughts about each other; yet they both love each other. Their egos seem to be in charge, with neither one wanting to make the first move toward resolving the estrangement. Life is too short to have this bad feeling in the family."

Melanie, Wilma's ten year old daughter, overheard the conversation. "Mommy, I think Grandma just needs to chill out and play nice with Uncle Wally. After all, he is her son. You're always so nice to me; unless I do something really bad like cut my new jeans into shorts. Why can't Grandma be the same with Uncle Wally? She's your mom and she's nice to you. I don't get why she can't be nicer to Uncle Wally. And I think Uncle Wally should be kinder to Grandma. Both of them just need to chill out, and make up," Melanie concluded with childlike certainty.

Wilma was left very thoughtful by her daughters' perception. Melanie was right on the money. Seen from her youthful perspective, it seemed a simple thing to "chill out and make up." Could it be that simple?

The next morning Wilma called her brother. "Is it okay with you if we continue our conversation about Mom?"

"Sure, I guess so," Wally said, unenthusiastically.

"Have you taken Mom for a car ride recently?"

"No, I haven't. We end up snapping at each other, so I haven't bothered."

"Would you be willing to try again, Wally? I have a hunch it would mean the world to her, and ultimately, to you. If you don't bite when she presses your red buttons, she may give it up. At the very least, you will feel better if you don't challenge her back; love her for who she is, our mother."

"It sounds pretty farfetched to me; and it also doesn't sound fair. Why shouldn't I react to her snapping at me? It feels like I'd be letting her get away with murder—the murder of my self-esteem!"

"Has snapping back helped your relationship?"

"No, but that's not the point."

"Think about what you just said, Wally. Consider if your behavior toward Mom is of service to the both of you. That's all I'm going to say about this. It's up to you now."

"What should I do?"

"I think you know the answer to that, Wally."

Wilma contemplated calling her mother to share what Wally was going through. She knew she was really sticking her nose into their business, but felt Harriet and Wally were on the edge of a new look at their relationship. On the way to work, she found herself driving by her mother's place, and before she could think about it, she parked and headed for the front door.

Her mother's face looked tired and fraught with worry when she answered the door. Hugging her affectionately, Wilma kept her arm around Harriet as they moved into the kitchen. Pouring her daughter a cup of coffee, Harriet asked, "What brings you here so early?"

"I thought I'd share with you what Wally and I have been talking about. Are you interested?"

"I guess so."

Wilma had to chuckle inside herself. Talk about two peas in a pod. Her mother and brother were so alike. Perhaps that was part of the problem. Neither wanted to give in; yet each appeared willing to consider it, if the other gave in first.

Wilma related to her mom how much Wally wanted the two of them to have a healthy relationship, but wasn't sure how to go about it. "What about you, Mom? Do you want to have a better relationship with Wally?"

Harriet stared at her daughter in consternation. "Of course I do. What do you take me for? I love my son. I just don't know how to be with him. Every time I say something, he snaps at me."

This time, Wilma couldn't help a chuckle escaping. "You both have the same story," she said with a twinkle in her eye. "Just be open, and change the story."

"What do you mean?"

"The next time you two talk, bring a positive feeling to your dialogue. When you find the conversation getting bogged down, be still for a moment until the feeling passes; don't retaliate. That is, if you don't want the unpleasant feeling to continue. I'll say it again; go for the positive feeling. That's how you'll change the story of your relationship with your son."

As Wilma resumed her drive to work, she called Wally on her cell phone and related the gist of her chat with their mother. "It's up to you and Mom now, Wally. I'm out of the middle. Good luck! I know you both can come to peace if you keep your hearts in the right place."

"I appreciate all you've done, Wilma. You've certainly earned your sister and daughter stripes. You've been promoted to Family Mediator."

"No thank you!" Wilma declared. They both burst out laughing, and clicked off the cell phone.

Wilma felt hopeful that both Harriet and Wally had realized something deeper about emotions and stress; emotions are ageless, and so is stress. They occur at any age, with any gender. As long as we have the power to think, we have the power to change. It remained to be seen how mother and son would shape their new story. Perhaps it would be beyond their imaginations, creating a new reality for both.

Enjoying the Simple Things in Life

One of the favorite things Ken and I love to do, especially on a sunny day, is go for a drive around the island. Spring is starting to proudly display its splendor; the hawthorn trees and wild rose bushes are unfurling fresh green leaves that look almost translucent. Cedar and other evergreen branches, their new growth colored various shades of green, expand into the fullness of their beauty. Brilliant yellow broom blossoms peek out from within their nests of greenery.

As we leisurely wind our way around the narrow country roads, we come to a meadow with sheep wandering here and there. Little lambs frolic about, looking as if they have springs in their legs, leaping into the air for nothing more than pure joy. Another two wee ones lie sleeping near the fence, nestled close, one resting its head on the other's belly. Their mother stands protectively nearby, contentedly munching grass.

We drive on, quietly enjoying the scenery, grateful to be living on this beautiful island. We sniff appreciatively, as the fragrance of a fire burning old branches and other debris from the winter season comes to our attention; the result of someone's spring yard work. The deep feeling of contentment is alive and well, as we enjoy the simple pleasures life has to offer.

Many times in the past, our lives weren't so peaceful; contentment was a rare emotion in our world. Rather, stress and anxiety were the norm, our reality filled with various complications.

Some were real, and some we made up. Either way, we didn't know how to nourish the deeper feelings of appreciation. More to the point, we didn't even realize there were deeper feelings, or unconditional feelings of gratitude, or of happiness.

Could this be what life is all about, uncovering the source of happiness? Could this be what being in the moment means? Is it enjoying the simple pleasures of nature? Is it re-discovering new meaning in long time relationships that makes them fresh, new and exciting? Is being in the moment accepting life's challenges and seeing the challenges as opportunities to grow?

These are questions to ponder, questions to be answered by our deeper self. Most times I answer a resounding "yes." Other times, depending on my state of mind, I answer with a degree of uncertainty. However, the ambiguity does not feel good, and then I know I am off track, and not in the moment. That *knowing* takes me to the present, where once again I live life the best I can.

One of the things I appreciate most about knowing we all have happiness within us is the gentleness this knowledge brings to life. I find I am less judgmental about myself and others. The kindness and resiliency of mental health constantly reaffirms itself, if we allow it to do so.

I recall the words that Syd spoke to me, about happiness being inside; the memory of those words has never left me. I admit, the meaning behind the phrase has been covered by negative thinking numerous times. The thinking could be judgment about a family member, or having expectations rather than acceptance. It could be impatience with how life should unfold. It could be the thought that in order to be happy, you have to have a certain person in your life, or out of your life.

Sooner or later, if you let it, inner wisdom arises once more, and the realization that happiness is unconditional settles you down again. This is when the answers, to whatever is unsettling you, come. This is when you understand more fully that uncovering your spiritual core is what brings true, lasting happiness.

"How do I keep the feeling of happiness alive?" I've been asked that question countless times; perhaps a few days or weeks after people have attended Three Principles training. They will tell me how incredible they felt while enveloped in the beautiful spiritual feeling the seminar and speakers appeared to have drawn out of them.

My response is to point out that the deep feeling they experienced comes from them. The speakers may be the catalyst; but ultimately, it is their own wisdom within that is being stirred. "Yes, I know that, but how do I keep that feeling alive?" is the comeback.

I repeat; the feeling of love, warmth, and stillness is coming from you! The actual feeling is generated by your true self. The more you realize that, the more spiritual power you gain to help further your inner growth; this keeps the feeling alive.

Continue uncovering your true identity; layer by layer, or a few at a time. Each layer peeled off reveals more beauty, contentment, stability, and deep appreciation for all life has to offer. It's like having the veil that appears to separate the inner and the outer world dissolve, revealing the Oneness.

Enjoy your life; relish the simple pleasures of your everyday existence. Embrace life as the wee lambs frolicking in the field, leaping in the air, simply enjoying being alive. You may find your favorite things are the simple pleasures life has to offer.

Happiness From Within

*M*uch of the world looks for happiness through achievements. For example, a student may think, "If I pass this test, I'll be happy. If I don't, I'm doomed." While the student is stressed, he or she is not thinking clearly, is apt to find studying difficult, and may be unable to retain information. Consequently, a self-fulfilling prophecy occurs; the student does not make the grade.

On the other hand, a student who is feeling mentally healthy is relaxed, confident, finds studying interesting and enjoyable, and may well ace the test. Even if the student doesn't do well on the test, chances are he or she will roll with the punches and come out the other side, understanding that failure can be a step toward success, if you don't judge yourself for failing.

A similar pitfall for people who are familiar with the Three Principles is the trap of judging themselves or others when they slip out of a healthy state of mind. People often think that once you gain a degree of understanding of the Principles, life becomes a bed of roses. Such is not the case. Certainly, life becomes much more balanced, enriched and enjoyable; but there are still times when one experiences difficult situations. If you see yourself as a life-long student and view every circumstance as an opportunity to continue learning, you are granted amnesty from negativity, for the most part.

It's all in the way one thinks about life's occasional challenges. Even when wisdom is guiding you away from a negative situation, you may still find fault with yourself for falling into a low state. Judging and finding fault perpetuate the condition. If you're judging others, that hurts you more than those you are judging.

What I suggest is that people cultivate and nourish the feeling of gratitude. Gratefulness brings gentleness into your life. When you're not so hard on yourself, you're not so hard on others. Gratitude is an attribute of well-being. This deep feeling brings understanding, and solutions to the issues one may be struggling with. It also brings compassion for those who are stressed; helping you see it is their unhappiness causing them to be negative or harsh toward others.

The simplicity and power of well-being brings an inner happiness that does not depend on anything in the outer world. In other words, this kind of inner contentment is unconditional. While well–being is a profound quality, it is also very practical. There is nothing that isn't touched and affected by well-being; new opportunities seem to come out of the blue. It may be that a new job is offered, a prospective client calls, a long deserved vacation becomes possible, or a new friend appears; a kindred spirit on the same inner journey. These occasions make it look like good fortune is coming your way. In the true reality, living in mental health is what brings this "good fortune."

Happiness draws people to you, people who feel your inner peace. It may be the new client, a colleague, a grocery clerk, your hair stylist or barber, a server in a restaurant; people with whom you engage in meaningful conversation, be it for a minute or an hour. Of course, your family benefits simply by osmosis, as well as in moments of deeper connection, whether spoken or unspoken. These moments of communication are precious, something to be cherished. Each one is an example of your true self, recognizing the mystical connection with another soul.

Divine Energy is the spiritual essence we're made of. It manifests in a feeling of well-being; a feeling that "all is right with the world" even when it doesn't look that way, in terms of the global experience. When you live in a feeling of peace and calm, there is a spiritual ripple into the world that helps soothe the troubles that are paramount. It's a mystery how this happens; a gentle mystery.

The very least one's peace of mind offers to others is the refusal to judge what is wrong with the world. Judgment mires one in negative details. Rather, it is best to look at what is right. From this position, you see beyond the forest of doubt, of chaos, and can shine a light on the inner beauty that lies within each and every one.

The very best one can offer by living in well-being is to be an example; inspiring others to do the same. Ultimately, humanity will reach a point in consciousness that will bring peace, harmony, and alignment to the world. It starts with One.

Eliminate the Middle Man

$\mathcal{H}$ave you ever noticed how often we talk about "working" on our relationships, our marriage, our communication skills, even "working" on our tolerance. We're taught to work at our education, to work toward career advancement. It's as if we think we have to constantly improve in order to be accepted, by ourselves and by others.

What if I told you that "working" on issues is completely unnecessary? As a matter of fact, if you "work" on improving, you actually get in the way of enhancing your life, naturally. It sounds like avoidance, I know—but it isn't. "Working" at improving is, in reality, the middle man. It's an impediment to your true identity, covering up the source of enrichment. Go directly to the source, the Three Principles.

It's a spiritual fact; the deeper we go into understanding the Three Principles, the more our lives are enriched, automatically and natu rally. These Principles lead us into harmony and away from stress, once we realize that wisdom is nestled deep in our soul. Wisdom is hidden by the intellect, yet its presence fills every pore of our being.

This spiritual unfolding from within is our birthright. As Sydney Banks says in *The Missing Link*, page 31, *"All human beings have the inner ability to synchronize their personal mind with their impersonal mind to bring harmony into their lives."*

What an amazing gift— to know there is absolutely no need to "work" on issues. What a relief! I think of all the time Ken and I wasted, in the early days, working on our marriage. We focused on what was wrong, rather than being grateful for what was right. Now, I can see why we didn't get anywhere, except deeper in the hole!

We had no idea that such a consideration, seeing the good in each other, would nurture our relationship, bringing forth love and compassion. Yes, we did see the good in each other some of the time; that's how we fell in love. But much too soon, we tried to change each other, as we saw things we didn't like. Before we knew it, we were both consumed with what was wrong. This carried on until we learned about the Principles from Syd Banks.

During my early resistance to the Principles, I disliked the idea of being responsible for my reality. My world appeared as such a mess; how could I bear the thought that I had created this turmoil? When we had occasion to visit with Syd and his wife, Barb, despite my confusion and closed-mindedness to the Principles, I experienced a feeling of lightness, of *joie de vivre*. My struggle was non-existent, for that period of time.

As I relaxed, I would feel inclined to ask Syd questions about how the Principles worked. I would ask his advice about the problems Ken and I had. Smiling, and shaking his head, he refused to be drawn into any discussion about issues. He would tell us not to fill our heads with perceived problems, but to appreciate each other. I can remember thinking, "These problems are real, not perceived."

Nonetheless, when my intellect wasn't occupied with working on a solution, the problems seemed to disappear. How could that be? Did the evaporation of whatever crisis we were experiencing have something to do with thought? Did it have something to do with a shift in our level of consciousness? Did it have something to do with not working on our problems, with not holding the issues so firmly in our minds? These questions lingered in my consciousness, long after our visit with the Banks' was over.

Recently, Ken and I were having a morning walk in the woods, filled with peace and appreciation for our beautiful surroundings. I shared with Ken my thoughts about our early days with the Banks' and how precious our time with them had been. He agreed, remarking how fortunate we were to have met Syd when we did. Had we not, likely we would have divorced.

We stopped to rest on a log, overlooking the ocean, and spotted the ferry heading from Fulford dock en route to Victoria. We reminisced about our dating and early years together. It floored us as we realized, after five decades of marriage, how compatible we were when we were first dating. I had memories of arguments, of breaking up countless times because we didn't get along; or so I thought. Yet, when we looked back, we realized we'd loved being together most of the time, and loved being alone with each other. One of our favorite outings was going for long drives on rough logging roads, feeling adventurous, as if we were pioneers. We enjoyed quiet time, being in nature, even then.

Where was my head, during those early years, thinking only with dissatisfaction, of what I didn't have? My mind had been full of negative thoughts about my needs not being met, feeling my happiness depended on Ken. Now, I see that my happiness comes from within me, from discovering who and what I really am—a spiritual being, like everyone else on this planet.

My past has changed, as if by magic, from one of unhappiness to one of contentment. I look at Ken and see with pleasure that he is happier than ever before. It's as if the past has evaporated into the mists of time and beautiful memories crop up. Yes, if I want to, I can still recall incidents that were troublesome and stressful. But I view them with love and understanding, knowing we were innocently lost in the form of life. And I find that those memories simply aren't in my consciousness anymore; so why would I want to bring them back?

To find each other within the spiritual realm, connecting soul to soul, is a treasure beyond compare. Welcome to a world where "working" on improving yourself is unimportant. Welcome to a world of grace and ease. Welcome to the world within.

Trust Your Own Wisdom

Our birthright is innate mental health, which is another name for innate wisdom. The wisdom we are born with is not of this world. Wisdom is from the spiritual realm, before the form of our world. Occasionally, our natural wisdom is covered up by our concerns about life, by not trusting that when we live life in alignment with our true self, we are taken care of. This is true in whatever situation we may find ourselves.

As practitioners, all we need to do is point our clients in the direction of their own wisdom. When we do that, rather than trying to "fix" them, we give them hope that they have the personal power to help themselves. When people get a glimmer of this spiritual fact, they get a deep feeling of well-being, which is wisdom expressing itself. The feeling of well-being is what heals people spiritually, from the inside-out.

In *The Hawaii Lectures* DVD, *Oneness of Life*, Sydney Banks says *"You're all sitting here enlightened—you just don't know it."* I've listened to that recording for years but I couldn't quite "hear" what he was saying. His declaration was too powerful for me to absorb. Recently, I happened to play his DVD again. This time I was able to hear his emphatic statement a bit more; the words seemed to emerge from my soul. I *see* that innate mental health is part of enlightenment. All we need to do is open up to "what is."

Consider the implications of this new paradigm of mental health. When people present their issues to us, as practitioners, we listen with respect and empathy. Then, a moment occurs when we know that to listen any more to the details of the problem only reinforces the problem. When we, as helpers, go "home" to our own wisdom, by the very nature of that process, we invite our clients home as well.

When we are strong in what we know, that we are spiritual beings living in a physical reality, we don't tend to get caught up in the "story" of others' realities or even our own reality. We begin to see the illusionary nature of life. Evidence of the illusionary nature of life is *seeing* how our experience changes as our thinking changes. By wisely using the Principles of Mind, Consciousness and Thought, our reality continues to improve, naturally.

I know there are many in the world dedicated to helping those who are living in wretched circumstances, and I applaud their efforts. I also know that you can help people change the form of their reality and effectively help transform their lives. The larger picture of permanent, sustainable change must come from a shift in the world's level of consciousness. When that spiritual shift happens, the atrocities that are occurring will begin to diminish, because people who are mentally healthy lead healthy lives.

Countless people who have committed various crimes and ended up in prison have been introduced to the Principles and had a shift in their level of consciousness that changed their lives. A man who continues to serve time for manslaughter has embraced the Principles and exemplifies to other inmates how to live with hope, despite their incarceration. He is a role model for finding peace of mind while confined.

What does this tell us? That it is never too late to change; that wisdom moves in mysterious ways, helping those less fortunate to become fortunate; that there is more to life than the form of life. There is something beyond the form that we are all part of, where we are One.

An example comes to mind of how wisdom emerges when we allow time and space. Last summer, after I conducted a seminar for a group, a participant asked to meet with me later that day for a private session. I hesitated, wanting to be of service, and then to my surprise these words came out of me. "Take the time for your own wisdom to emerge. Frankly, I feel the same need for myself, time to absorb all that occurred during the seminar, and time for new insights to manifest."

The participant was gracious in accepting my response, and I offered to talk with him at a future date. A couple of weeks later, I heard from the individual; he said he had gained much knowledge in that time of private reflection. He commented on how powerful it was to realize it was his own wisdom coming to light, not mine.

At the same seminar, another individual asked to see me privately. Her particular needs tugged at my heartstrings, so I agreed. When I met with her the next day, she wanted to talk about her problems. Instead, I talked with her about the spiritual nature of life, encouraging her to trust her own innate wisdom to resolve her difficulties. I could see she wanted to believe what I was saying, even while she struggled with it; but I gently and respectfully refused to entertain her "story."

I felt a peace come over me as I held to the truth that nothing is resolved by focusing on the problems. We sat in silence for some time. I could feel her calm down as we experienced the feeling of peace together. After a time, she stood up and quietly said, "Thanks, Elsie. I feel the truth of what you are saying. The quiet time we just spent moved me out of my problem solving dilemma. I don't understand exactly how, but I feel it."

Her words struck a chord in me. It's so true; we don't have to understand exactly how the Principles work. As a matter of fact, we never will understand them intellectually. As Syd said many times, we are already enlightened; we just need to realize it. And we do; every time we have an insight, it comes from that place, again in Syd's words, "beyond time, space and matter."

The Nature of Addictions

Over the years, I've often been asked about substance abuse and addictions. The two questions below have come up often, and I feel it may be helpful to answer them as best as I can. I am not an addictions counsellor, but I worked for a number of years with an organization that offered traditional addictions programs, based on the disease model.

First question: "Do you have to give up your traditional addictions programs in order to fully follow the Three Principles? Or can you do both at the same time?"

Answer: You don't have to give up anything you don't want to. I observed that clients in substance abuse programs often found a wonderful sense of freedom, once they were introduced to the Three Principles. This freedom came from realizing they were mentally healthier than they'd thought; they began to *see* they had a default capacity for innate wisdom they could depend on, to consistently guide them to a safe home "inside" themselves.

As mentioned, the organization I worked with offered the traditional disease model, among many other programs. I was brought in because the CEO was intrigued by the new paradigm of the Three Principles, which is based on seeing innate mental health in individuals, rather than dysfunction.

One of the groups I worked with there consisted of addictions counsellors and their clients. Sometimes the staff had more difficulty accepting the Principles than the clients did. This is because the staff were caught up in the form of their program and were occasionally hesitant to change to something new.

Innate wisdom, another term for innate mental health, is a relatively new concept. Innate wisdom is that inner spark that helps heal addictions; an inner spark of divinity that can never be extinguished. When that inner spark is released, amazing things happen. People find hidden strength that helps them resolve the challenges they face. They become hopeful and optimistic, realizing it is never too late to change, to find fulfilment and purpose. They discover that life is filled with beauty and joy.

Something else I observed in my work with addictions is that when people tap into their inner wisdom, coupled with learning about the true nature of the Principles and how we use them to create our personal experience, the thinking of the individual is improved, via insight. It's not a forced "reframing" but a natural unfolding of the wisdom within, leading to understanding that moves one past addiction. Once the "thought'" of addiction decreases, the need also decreases. I've seen people naturally move away from addictions, because they have found solace, peace and happiness within.

Second Question: "Are there any areas where the Three Principles would disagree with religion?"

Answer: The Three Principles understanding directs people to the spiritual essence of life, before the form and dogma of religion. If you find solace in religion, then keep going; do what feels right to you. Sydney Banks, the originator of these Principles, experienced the pure formless energy before form. He told us that this formless energy can be called many things. Some call this spiritual energy God, Divine Mind, and so on. Whatever you call it, it is the spiritual energy of all things, both the form and the formless.

To me, the main point is seeing there is something before the physical form of life and nature; something greater, that we are part of. It is *seeing* that we are, at the core, spiritual beings, carrying that divine spark within us. We *are* that divine spark. Oftentimes we cover it up with our personal thinking, but it is always there. Our journey in life is to uncover our true identity and live life as it is meant to be lived; with peace of mind and contentment. This is our birthright. Our life transforms as we honor and cherish this birthright.

Sydney Banks, in his DVDs, CDs and books, gives a far better description of the true nature of life than is found here. I encourage you to embrace these resources. There is no question that Syd's materials are the best place to find the deepest answers. They have the power to awaken that which lies deep within, allowing all the answers we seek to be revealed, via our own wisdom.

Another Dimension

One sunny spring day, as I was enjoying my morning coffee on our backyard patio, I marveled that my surroundings felt like an oasis. The quiet murmur of water, rippling over the decorative stones in the fountain, soothed my mind. I noticed the interplay of sun and shade on the laburnum tree in the corner; its soft, yellow blossoms hanging in a graceful cluster, amidst delicate, fern like leaves.

Until the sun illuminated it, the tree had been in shadow, with beautiful, subtle patterns playing over its foliage. Then as the sun spread its rays, they brought to light another dimension of the tree; more depth, intensified color, a radiant glow that brought the tree to life.

"It's like another dimension of us," is the phrase that flowered in my mind, as I observed the enhanced beauty of the laburnum. Just as the sun showed another dimension of the tree, the Principles lead us to, and illuminate, another dimension of ourselves.

As we discover an inner dimension of ourselves—our spiritual identity—we also begin to realize the gift of original thought, another term for innate wisdom or insight. This is a marvelous gift that allows us to create a wondrous world.

As I continued to sip my coffee, I heard, before I saw, two hummingbirds performing aerial acrobatics in the sky. Unbelievably swift, faster at times then the eye can see, their wings beat about fifty five times per second.

Our thoughts also travel faster than the eye can see, sometimes spinning out of control. Before I was introduced to the Principles, my mind was so busy I couldn't rest; I always had to have something on the go. When I first heard Sydney Banks talk about peace of mind, I couldn't imagine ever achieving such a state in this lifetime.

As I reminisced, I remembered a conversation with Celia, a woman who was deeply depressed, and had been for some time. She had contacted me for some private coaching sessions, which I provided for her on Salt Spring Island. After doing some intake, I shared the Principles with her, and played Syd's DVDs, but she was having a very difficult time grasping anything because her mind was so busy. She constantly analyzed everything I said.

Celia was consumed with worry. Her questions concerned the past, the present, and the future. At one point, I asked her if worrying helped her in any way. "I'm not really worrying," she responded, "I'm just wondering about what to do."

"Isn't wondering also thought?" I asked Celia. We had already discussed the role of thought in creating our experience, and how worrying or wondering about things we couldn't help did not serve us well. "These thoughts cloud over the wisdom that is waiting to guide us through life."

"I don't know what you mean by that. I don't know what to do."

"Live in the moment, the best you can. Appreciate what you have, rather than focusing on what you don't have. The more you live in the moment, the quieter your mind will become."

She was just about to reply to that when I said, "Let's forget about the Principles for now and I'll take you to visit the art galleries in the village."

Celia hesitated. "I didn't come here to tour art galleries."

"Trust me, Celia. Perhaps you will learn more about yourself as you enjoy the art. Or if you prefer, we can go for a drive and appreciate the beauty of the island."

Celia did relax a bit, but I could see her mind was still going in circles. We spent time together over the course of several days, and each time she had more and more questions. I shared my story about my own depression in the early years of my marriage. I related how getting a glimmer of understanding of the Principles helped move me into another dimension of reality; a reality where the shadows of depression lifted, to reveal a life filled with light, peace, and contentment.

"That's fine for you, Elsie; but I can't stop my thinking. It feels out of control. I don't know what to do," she repeated.

"I know it seems difficult to get your thinking under control, Celia. You're trying so hard. And that's part of the problem. Just relax and let it go. Your mental health will rise to the surface when you relax. If you hang onto your negative thoughts, they will be reflected in your life. You have the power to let go of those thoughts; let them slip away, like the shadows in the night as day breaks."

"What will be left, if I let go of my thinking?" was her earnest plea for help.

"Peace," I replied.

Celia's face stilled as her wisdom began to emerge. I could see the light begin to dawn in her eyes; yet, several times she tried to articulate her concern about letting go of her personal anxiety. But she could no longer express her habitual negative thoughts. It was as if she had experienced a "short" in her negative thinking, as if the fuse had been blown.

Various emotions chased each other across her face. Finally, with a note of wonder in her voice, she said, "Can it really be that simple? Can I find relief from my depression, simply by pointing myself in the direction of positivity? All the therapy I've been through has focused on my problems, and you're telling me to 'relax' and my 'mental health will emerge.' I don't know what to make of it. I want to believe you. I sense there is something to what you are saying; but it's completely different from what I'm used to."

Comprehension continued to grow on Celia's face as she realized the truth. Negative thoughts are the core of depression; let them drift away, and you move beyond depression into another reality, a whole new world.

"You make is sound so simple," she said again, and sighed.

I knew she had opened the door to her own wisdom, and her journey from then on would be a more positive one. Once the door to wisdom is opened, there is no going back. Wisdom is too powerful, and the feeling of light and openness is too appealing. No longer are you hidden under a shadow.

Celia's wistful questions brought back more memories of my past. I was brought up in the '50's when the "cold war" was still a reality. At school, we were taught to hide under a desk, should a bomb go off. Of course, as children, we were filled with excitement at the possibility that this could occur. We weren't really afraid, just filled with the drama of it all.

Once I married and had children of my own, I did become very concerned about the state of the world. In the mid-sixties, the United States was waging war in Vietnam, and I wondered, just like Celia, what would happen. I pondered on what would happen to our children; I worried about how we would survive if a war came to Canada. I worried myself sick.

To prepare for the worst, Ken and I bought a hundred pounds of rice and a hundred pound pail of honey. We were told these were good, long lasting food items. We ended up eating these products for years. It turned me off rice for quite some time. . .

Now I can laugh at our actions, but before I *saw* the role of thought in creating the human experience, I was a victim of my own negative thoughts. Once I realized that thoughts create feelings, I saw my anxious thoughts for what they were; just thoughts, out of control. *Seeing* regulated my thoughts in a healthy manner.

Please understand; I'm not making light of using common sense to protect your family and yourself. I'm saying, use thought wisely. Don't use the power of thought against yourself—to create worry.

As Sydney Banks says in his book, *The Missing Link*, p.102, *"We must rid ourselves of yesterday's negative thoughts to receive today's new and positive feelings."*

Magical Moments

A slight haze covered the hills, softening their outline, and presenting a mystical background to the sea in front. Ken and I sat in our comfortable camping chairs, observing the diverse vessels traversing Ganges Harbor. There were yachts, sailboats, old fishing trawlers converted into comfortable living quarters, and dinghies coming and going from the village to their crafts. The salt tang of sea air added to our enjoyment as we breathed in, filling our lungs with life and vitality. It was a magical moment, bringing us fresh appreciation, not only for the beautiful view in front of us, but for life in general.

The insight gained from catching a glimmer of the nature of the Principles, and of life, brings freedom of mind to enjoy and cherish the limitless bounty our environment offers. This quality of *seeing* brings luminosity to everything we view. All appears imbued with energy; richer, with more vibrant color, seeming to shimmer in the light. Satisfying to the eye and the soul, you can gently feel nature, life, and true self merging into One.

These magical moments illuminate the connection between all things. Difficult to describe, but once such moments are experienced, all life is enriched. Understanding the true nature of humanity is enhanced, leading to more harmony, leading to deeper exploration of who and what we really are.

Hearing a noise brought me from my reverie. Glancing up, I noticed a man coming down the stairs behind us. He was wearing work clothes and carrying a mug of coffee; its fragrance drifted toward us as he approached our chairs. "Hi there. Enjoying the view?" he asked.

"Very much," Ken replied. We started to chat and before we knew it, a beautiful feeling of connection developed between us. We talked about how grateful we were to live on such a beautiful island, with clean air and water. In a few minutes of conversation, he told us much about himself, private things. We learned he had left his well-paying job in another province because of the level of stress involved. Now he works outdoors in the fresh air, gets less pay, but works fewer hours. The conversation ended with all of us agreeing there was more to life than money.

After he left, Ken and I both felt a strong sense of community with the stranger. He was unknown to us, but in that brief moment of rapport, we discovered a kindred spirit. We *saw* him and he *saw* us. We marveled at how a spontaneous exchange can feel profound. It was an ordinary occurrence; yet, a magical moment.

The sound of a float plane captured our attention. We watched the pilot make a picture perfect landing and smoothly taxi up to the dock. It appeared effortless; as effortless as our consciousness lifting, filling us with peace and utter contentment.

The gift of *seeing* is a natural outcome of releasing our true self from within. This divine core contains the complete package, implanted with Three Principles that lead us to wisdom, that lead us deeper into the unity of all things. Isn't it incredible to know we already *are* what we seek?

Seeing shows up in so many unexpected ways—*seeing* the stranger as a kindred spirit, *seeing* the beauty around us, *seeing* connection as spiritual. *Seeing* enhances everything. It bears repeating: *Seeing* is our natural default setting.

There are many layers to *seeing*; not everyone sees things in the same way. As we continue to evolve, our own *seeing* advances and matures; although occasionally, I admit, *seeing* seems to recede. Sometimes it appears a wonder we are able to communicate with each other at all, given the separate realities we experience.

The common denominator underlying humanity is that we are all spiritual beings. The tricky part is, you can get gripped by the physical form. This stops you from seeing *"what is, rather than what isn't."* This is a quote from Sydney Banks, who made this statement many times. I was always puzzled by this and wondered what on earth he meant. I still wonder! But the feeling now is wondrous rather than confusion.

The other day, I had a conference call with a group. During the call, I experienced deep moments of connection, magical moments. The attentive silence at the other end of the line told me the group was with me. Then there were moments when I felt unconnected and couldn't tell what the group was feeling.

It was a bit of a whirlwind; different levels of consciousness being experienced in the blink of an eye. The call left me thoughtful and introspective. Thankfully, I was able to defuse my personal thinking by going to that quiet place inside. In that space, I found peace.

In the middle of the night, I was awakened by my thinking, going a mile a minute. Again, I was taken on a spin. Somehow, in the midst of the ride, wisdom emerged; mystical in nature, the moment offered comfort and solace.

That morning I received an email from a member of the group. To my delight, I read that they felt the talk was insightful and had facilitated their connection as a team. The conversation they had, following our discussion, helped them coalesce beyond the separate realities they had been experiencing. They were *seeing* each other differently, seeing beyond the disguise of their work titles and positions. The email message cleared my eyes to see beyond my interpretation of what had happened during the call. Once again, it was a shift in understanding for all of us.

Time and again, a shift in consciousness happens, without effort, without doing anything; when we are simply "being."

Someone said to me the other day that learning about the Principles is like drinking from the fountain of knowledge, and constantly being replenished. The statement has a ring of infinity, of everlasting learning. How did we get so lucky to find this profound gift within?

Knowing who we are, at a core level, takes care of life forever more. That's all that's required. How simple and profound can you get? Then, life is filled with magical moments.

One Door Closes, Another Opens

*I*n the silence of my mind, a thought appeared; I wondered what the future would hold. With the passing of Sydney Banks in 2009, a phrase came to mind: "As one door closes, another opens."

It takes faith to be open to what the future holds, when the familiar is no longer accessible. "What now?" you ask yourself. It's easy to say, "Have faith." It's not always easy to *feel* faith. Certainly, the more we query the future, the less we are in the moment, where solace and answers await. In our uncertainty, it may seem we are back to square one; a student, only beginning to learn how to live.

It's a good place to be; a place of openness, a place of humility, a place of unknowing. The *knowing* will manifest when our mind becomes still. In the stillness is peace and harmony. Trust that whatever the future holds, it will bring learning, moving us forward to uncover our true identity.

Syd uncovered his true identity, spontaneously revealed to him in the moment. He wasn't looking for anything; as he often said, he didn't know there was anything to find. But when this miracle happened to him, he knew exactly what he had found. In his words, "*I know I've found the secret to life; I've found the true nature of God.*"

He welcomed his true self with supreme gratitude, and with passion and total commitment. Syd was an ordinary man who was blessed to receive an unparalleled gift that transformed him into an extraordinary man. Yet, Syd often spoke about the satisfaction of being ordinary.

I'd been ordinary all my life, so I wasn't enamored with his direction: "Be ordinary." He told us that once we'd had an insight, to just live, to be ordinary, and go about our everyday life. He said we'd see the world differently, that the many issues we were troubled by would become non-issues; he told us we'd have far more enjoyment with the simple things in life.

In those early days, I found this a bit perturbing. It's true my life had changed, but I was hanging on to the need to feel "special," not ordinary. The feeling was subtle, so subtle that I didn't see it for a while.

Misinterpreting and confusing the Principles' message of inner spiritual power, my ego's desire to be something special in this world soon brought me up short. I began to realize that being special was not all I thought it would be. The longer I hung on to that need, the less special I felt.

I recall, one autumn day many years ago, wandering down the back road to Syd's place to help him work on his first book, *Second Chance*. I observed a squirrel digging in the soil, diligently scooping through the leaves. He was hiding some nuts he'd found, a treasure for the future. It occurred to me in a flash of insight that I also was hiding a treasure—my innate wisdom. I was covering up my natural wisdom by my ego's need to be "special."

That revelation filled me with wonder and lifted my spirits to a height I had not experienced before. My need to feel special evaporated like the mist in the morning sun. I realized we all are born special—from birth to death—we are spiritual beings privileged to create and live in the beautiful form of life.

To realize we have the power to create our personal experience is a very special gift. It's our divine birthright. You can't get anything more special than that gift. This knowledge struck me with such depth. I understood for the first time that living an ordinary life, walking down a country lane, could be transformed into a magical journey. As my spirits and level of consciousness lifted, my observations of the physical world around me were enhanced. It was as if I'd never seen such beauty, such a deep dimension of nature; alive, pulsating with vitality.

I arrived at Syd's door, knocked and was invited to enter. Syd gave me a hug as I stood before him. He took one look at my face and grinned from ear to ear. *"Something has happened to you. You look as if you've received a Christmas present and birthday present all rolled into one."*

I shared with him my experience, my need to feel special and how I hadn't liked his encouragement to be "ordinary." Telling him about the insight I'd had as I walked down the country lane and how my vision of the surrounding environment was enriched, I felt overcome with emotion and had to stop.

He chuckled as he listened. *"You've finally entered a new reality, the mystical world of true knowledge, where everything becomes new again. The most ordinary things in life take on more meaning; you feel fresh appreciation, both for your surroundings and for your family and friends. Continue to be grateful for what you've just seen and you'll never go wrong. Gratitude is the lubricant for a happy life."*

Those words are imprinted upon my soul. I've never forgotten them and they stand me in good stead to this very day. Gratitude truly is the lubricant for a happy life. And in being "ordinary" and acknowledging our divine inheritance, we are "special" indeed.

I continued to work with Syd on his book, typing up draft after draft. In those early days, I had an old, manual Underwood typewriter. It was an exciting time, learning from Syd while I was typing his words. Most of what I typed was beyond my understanding; but nonetheless, his words stirred something deep within me. We would talk for hours about his writings; me striving to understand, Syd chuckling at my earnest attempt to comprehend the mystery of the indescribable.

"Don't try to figure it out, Elsie," Syd would tell me. *"Just enjoy the feeling, and the answers you seek will appear."*

I remember one day near Christmas, walking down a snow-covered country road from our home to Syd's. Tucked under my arm was the latest chapter I had typed for him. Cedar trees lining the road were bent with the weight of the snow, no tracks littered the lane, and the overcast sky held a promise of more flurries to come. It was a pristine scene; the unspoiled beauty of nature, magical in appearance; a winter wonderland. I saw none of it at the time.

As I walked, I ruminated on what the New Year would bring. Financially, Ken and I were close to the edge. I was definitely experiencing some angst. How would we manage? Where would the money come from? We couldn't afford much in the way of gifts for our children, or our friends.

Arriving at Syd's door, with a face looking like Scrooge, I just about uttered, "Baa, humbug," when he greeted me with a big smile, welcoming me into his cozy home with a warm, *"Merry Christmas, dearie."*

Holding back my words of woe, I handed the chapter to Syd and settled myself close to the fireplace. Cheerfully, he said, *"Oh, I've changed this chapter again. It's completely different."* He was delighted; I was not.

This happened countless times. I would finish typing his work, hand it to him, and he would inform me that it had changed once again. Back to the typewriter I'd go.

Little did I know then, that each time I typed it over, I learned something new. Not only that, but clearly Syd had found something new as well, in expressing what he wanted to say.

Those times of learning helped uncover my spiritual intelligence. Like the snow melting, releasing the landscape beneath, so did my personal thinking melt, releasing my inner wisdom. This new knowledge provided a higher vantage place, allowing me to *see* and *hear* how to live life in peace and harmony.

As I walked back home, my spirits lifted from working with Syd, I saw before me an incredibly beautiful scene, like a Currier & Ives Christmas card. My heart welled with gratitude at the opportunity offered me, to type his words, to be in his presence, to learn from an enlightened being.

Now, thirty-seven years later, the scene is as fresh in my mind as if it took place yesterday. The opportunity we all have to continue learning from Sydney Banks' missives of hope and transformation is truly beyond our imagination.

After Syd's passing, Ken and I, as so many others, felt bereft without Syd's presence on this earth. How do we continue this work, sharing the profound and practical message that Syd left the world? How do we find our own voice? How do I find my voice?

I wasn't sure of anything, save that the Three Principles will never die; they are beyond this world of form, and are everlasting. To know there is such a lasting gift, from generation to generation, is beyond reassuring. Suffice to say, I have the strongest inner sense that this is so. Time will tell.

What I do know, is that many people I consider pioneers in the Three Principles community, have found their way deeper into their own wisdom, which is helping preserve the legacy Syd left behind. The gift of true knowledge, the gift that never stops giving.

The new generations, sprouted from families who found their inner core, share their wisdom, supporting the previous generation, as well as adding their own mark. The cycle continues, the circle is unbroken, truth cannot be denied. Humanity does have the power to change, to live in peace and harmony, finding purpose, being of service—if they want. The answer is here, within us all.

One door has closed with Sydney Banks' absence; another has opened, drawing us deeper into our true nature, using our stronger, wiser voices, emerging into a new reality beyond our imagination, illuminating the way for future generations.

Epilogue

*I*t seems most appropriate to end this book by sharing my observations of the international conference that took place in London, Great Britain, June 2013. I feel this event was a pivotal moment in the manifestation of Sydney Banks' vision for the world.

After he experienced his epiphany revealing the Three Principles, Syd stated unequivocally that these Principles—Mind, Consciousness, and Thought—would change the fields of psychology and psychiatry, and would help alleviate human suffering.

Syd's realization heralded a totally new way of *seeing* mental health; every soul has the spiritual and mental resources "inside" making it possible to live in peace of mind and with well-being. Syd helped us *see* that it was unnecessary to focus on problems—that to do so actually escalated the issue. Instead, he pointed us to our inner wisdom, to our true nature, letting us know the answers reside inside our own psyche.

The conference opened by acknowledging Syd's gift to the world and his total dedication to sharing the foundational, spiritual Principles underlying the human experience.

The speakers at the conference spoke movingly of their own transformations, and related stories of their clients, who had suffered various mental disorders and traumas, finding hope and new meaning in their lives. Families who had been estranged told of coming together in peace and harmony. Stories were shared of inner city communities revitalized, homelessness issues addressed from understanding rather than despair, adult and adolescent corrections facilities sharing new learning on how to bring out the human potential in inmates, corporate executives finding new purpose and satisfaction in their personal and professional lives. All these examples and more were brought together under the umbrella of understanding the true nature of humanity; that we are spiritual beings living in a material world.

Ordinary people from every walk of life were in the audience, as well as mental health professionals from all areas of the field; psychologists, psychiatrists, physicians, counselors and a variety of service providers. A diversity of religious denominations, including many Rabbis and people of the Jewish faith, were also represented. Close to five hundred individuals from at least fifteen countries attended; truly a Three Principles "United Nations."

All came together in harmony, united in common purpose, to learn about "Change through Understanding the Three Principles," the theme of the conference. The feeling of love, respect, and consensus was palpable. Hope *is* alive and drawing people from around the world to share in the wonder.

It's not that there weren't questions asked and some confusion about what the Principles are and how they work; but the feeling of accord and unity, despite differences in language, culture, and religion, prevailed throughout the conference. It was a microcosm of what can happen in the world at large and what has happened already in inner city communities.

As a speaker at this event, I was constantly approached by participants who wished to share their experiences with me. The depth of feeling expressed by the participants ranged from hope for the human potential, to recognition of their divine essence that they had never felt before. Change and transformation happened before our very eyes, as people gained insight into the inner workings of their spiritual nature.

I visualized in each person a "pulsating ball of energy," similar to Syd's metaphor in the *Enlightened Gardener*, with beams of pure light and wisdom radiating out into the world; bringing a deeper degree of peace to creation, as all are enriched by this simple and natural understanding.

Sydney Banks, an ordinary man who had a profound extraordinary experience, left behind the legacy of the Three Principles, promising people that if they stepped "inside" and claimed their spiritual birthright, they would witness and contribute to a healing of the world as never seen before. It behooves us, and the global community, to support Syd in this directive; to honor our spiritual heritage.

Beyond imagination? Let's join together and dare to consider the possibility of peace and harmony uniting the world, and eventually, Syd's vision coming to fruition. A new era is dawning.

CPSIA information can be obtained
at www.ICGtesting.com
Printed in the USA
FSOW04n1952020615
7621FS